SEW-EASY
DESIGNER
BAGS &
TOTES™

Edited by Barbara Weiland

HOUSE of
WHITE
BIRCHFS
PUBLISHERS
SINCE 1947

SEW-EASY DESIGNER BAGS & TOTES

Copyright © 2006 House of White Birches, Berne, Indiana 46711

EDITOR	Barbara Weiland
ART DIRECTOR	Brad Snow
PUBLISHING SERVICES MANAGER	Brenda Gallmeyer
ASSOCIATE EDITOR	Dianne Schmidt
ASSISTANT ART DIRECTOR	Nick Pierce
COPY SUPERVISOR	Michelle Beck
COPY EDITORS	Nicki Lehman, Mary O'Donnell
TECHNICAL EDITOR	Barbara Weiland
TECHNICAL ARTIST	Nicole Gage
GRAPHIC ARTS SUPERVISOR	Ronda Bechinski
GRAPHIC ARTISTS	Glenda Chamberlain, Edith Teegarden
PRODUCTION ASSISTANTS	Cheryl Kempf, Marj Morgan
PHOTOGRAPHY	Tammy Christian, Don Clark, Christena Green, Matthew Owen, Jackie Schaffel
PHOTO STYLISTS	Tammy Nussbaum, Tammy M. Smith
HAIR & MAKEUP	Amy Isch
CHIEF EXECUTIVE OFFICER	John Robinson
PUBLISHING DIRECTOR	David J. McKee
EDITORIAL DIRECTOR	Vivian Rothe
MARKETING DIRECTOR	Dan Fink

Printed in China
First Printing: 2006
Library of Congress Control Number: 2005928352
Hardcover ISBN: 1-59217-092-7
Softcover ISBN: 1-59217-117-6

Every effort has been made to ensure the accuracy and completeness of the instructions in this book. However, we cannot be responsible for human error or for the results when using materials other than those specified in the instructions, or for variations in individual work.

1 2 3 4 5 6 7 8 9

Welcome!

Whether you call it a bag, a purse, a tote or a cloth runabout, any way you name it, a handbag is the perfect sewing project. Bags and totes don't require much fabric and most are easy to complete in just a few hours. Since there's no fitting, they offer frustration-free sewing. Can it get any better than that?

The projects in this book look expensive, but are easy to make for far less than you'd pay for similar bags in fine boutiques and department stores. Although most projects are small and don't take much time to sew, the results are eye-catching. Choose from dressy handbags, beautiful yet practical tote bags, glamorous purses for dress-up occasions and practical travel accessories—all in a variety of fabrics, sizes and shapes. You can make something totally girlie or totally functional or both. In fact, if you are in the habit of stashing away fabric like squirrels stash nuts in the fall, you probably already have the makings for several bags in your fabric and scrap stash. Cutting and sewing your own bags and totes offers a great opportunity to use up lining leftovers, zippers and the collection of creative embellishments that you've been hoarding for just the right project. And, there

just might be a beautiful fabric or two in the remnant bin at your favorite store, begging for a life as your favorite bag.

There are so many great projects, I'll bet you won't be able to stop at one! A quick trip to your favorite fabric or quilt shop should yield the special fabrics, assorted notions, embellishments and support materials you'll need to finish your bag and turn your sewing into a work of art that you'll be proud to carry and use.

Warm regards,

Barbara

Contents

TERRIFIC TOTES

BEAUTIFUL BAGS

ROMANTIC NOTIONS

NOVEL IDEAS

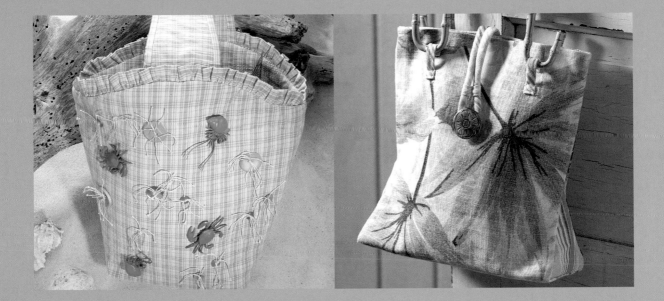

TERRIFIC TOTES

A girl can never have too many totes—for shopping, errands, trips to the beach—you name it. A tote is the perfect carryall for your necessities and your finds. Choose your favorite fabrics and trims to personalize the terrific totes that follow.

ALOHA FANTASY TOTE

DESIGN BY PAM LINDQUIST

This roomy lined bag is sure to be a summer favorite for shopping jaunts or trips to the beach. Tropical flowers cut from a bold print are the secret ingredient for this colorful tote.

FINISHED SIZE

14 x 18 inches, excluding straps

MATERIALS

- ¾ yard 44- or 54-inch-wide cotton canvas fabric for tote body
- Bold floral print for flower appliqués; yardage depends on the flower placement in the print you choose
- ⅝ yard accent fabric (bold stripe) for tote piping, straps and lining
- Synthetic suede scraps in red (or other color to match the flowers in the print)
- Scraps of green nonwoven synthetic suede for the leaves
- Fusible web
- 3⅞ yards narrow green ribbon
- Black all-purpose thread for stitched details
- All-purpose thread to match fabrics
- 2 decorative buttons for dimensional flower centers
- 1⅛ yards ⅛-inch-diameter cord for piping
- 3 yards ⅜-inch-diameter drapery cord for the handle
- 12 brass grommets with a ½-inch-diameter opening and grommet attachment tool
- Pattern tracing paper or cloth
- Pencil
- Air- or water-soluble marking pen
- Permanent black marking pen
- All-purpose thread to match fabrics
- Buttonhole twist or carpet thread
- Zipper foot
- Masking tape
- Bamboo skewer
- Rotary cutter, mat and ruler
- Sleeve board
- Basic sewing tools and equipment

INSTRUCTIONS

Project Note: *Use ½-inch-wide seam allowances.*

Cutting

- Enlarge the pattern (Figure 1) on pattern tracing paper or cloth.

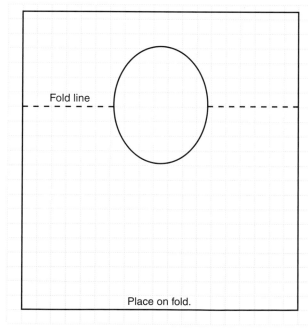

Fold line

Place on fold.

Figure 1
Aloha Tote Pattern
1 square = 1"

- From the canvas fabric, cut one tote body.
- From the accent fabric, cut two 8½ x 19-inch rectangles for the lining, plus one 1½ x 42-inch strip for the piping and enough 1¾-inch-wide bias strips to make a strip 100 inches long for the strap. Sew the bias strips together with bias seams and press them open.
- From the ribbon, cut three 42-inch-long pieces.
- From the print fabric, choose three flowers for the floral appliqués. One should be smaller than the others. Cut out the flowers, leaving extra margin beyond the edges so you have rectangles or squares to work with. Apply fusible web to the wrong side of each rectangle following the manufacturer's directions. Cut out the flowers along their outlines.
- On tracing paper, trace flower shapes for the flower centers. These should be smaller than the ones you chose for the appliqués. Cut out and use for patterns to cut the flowers from synthetic suede. Use a permanent marking pen to add flower details and outline the cut edges.

- On tracing paper, trace one or more leaf shapes from the floral print, or design your own. Use as patterns to cut the desired number of leaves from the green synthetic suede. Add veins and outline the edges with the marking pen.

Assembly

1. Draw ribbon-placement lines on the right side of the canvas tote panel. Position ribbons over the lines and stitch in place along each long edge (Figure 2).

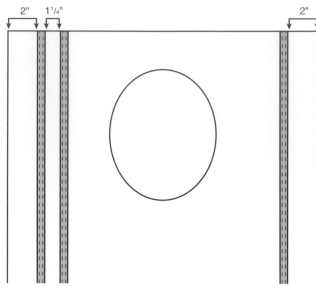

Figure 2
Mark positions for and sew ribbons to canvas.

2. Arrange the leaves and floral appliqué cutouts on the tote front as desired (see tote photo). Set the flowers aside and sew the leaves in place along the vein details with black thread. Remove the backing paper from the flowers, reposition them on the tote front and fuse in place following the manufacturer's directions. Satin-stitch over the raw edges with black thread.

3. Gather the center of each suede flower or pinch little pleats in it and tack in place on the canvas (Figure 3).

Figure 3
Gather flower centers.

4. Using buttonhole or carpet thread, sew the buttons in place on the flowers; sew through all layers for the most secure attachment.

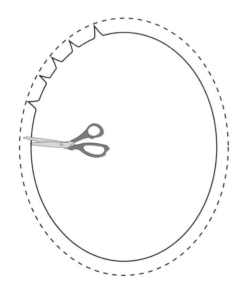

5. Machine baste ½ inch from the opening edges in the canvas. Clip the curves every ¼–½ inch (Figure 4). Turn under and press the raw edges, using the basting as a guide.

Figure 4
Machine-baste ¹/₂" from cutout edge. Clip to stitching.

6. Wrap the ⅛-inch-diameter cord with the 1½-inch-wide strip. Attach the zipper foot, adjust the needle to the left and stitch close to the cord to make piping. Trim the seam allowance to ½ inch from the stitching. Cut two 16-inch-long pieces from the piping.

7. Position the piping at the side edges of the canvas bag front, tapering the piping in at the upper and lower fold lines. Machine-baste in place (Figure 5). Trim the piping ends even with raw edges of the canvas as needed.

Figure 5
Sew piping to edges of tote between fold lines.

8. With right sides together, sew a lining piece to each short end of the canvas panel. Press the seam allowances toward the lining.

9. With right sides together and raw edges even, fold the tote body/lining panel in half. Stitch the side seams and press the seams open over a sleeve board. Turn under and press ½ inch around the bottom edge of the lining (Figure 6).

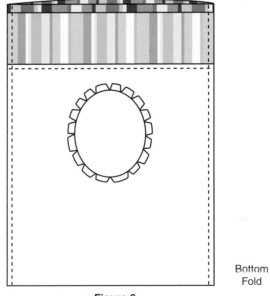

Bottom Fold

Figure 6
Sew tote/lining side seams.

14. At one end of the tube, turn under and push the raw edge up into the fabric tube about 1 inch. Wrap one end of the cord for the strap with masking tape. Insert the taped cord end into the turned fabric tube. Attach the cord to the fabric tube with a few hand stitches.

15. Use a bamboo skewer or other narrow turning tool to push the cord as far as it will go into the fabric tube (Figure 8). Remove the skewer.

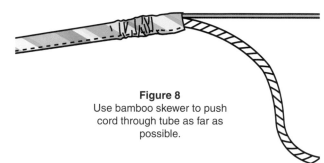

Figure 8
Use bamboo skewer to push cord through tube as far as possible.

10. Turn the bag right side out and edgestitch the turned edges of the lining together. Tuck the lining into the tote and press the upper edges of the canvas tote.

11. Slipstitch the folded edges of the opening together on each half of the bag. Edgestitch if desired.

12. Mark positions for the grommets, spacing them evenly around each opening edge. Attach the grommets following the directions for the attachment tool (Figure 7).

16. Hold firmly onto the taped cord end and gently coax the fabric tube to slide over the remaining cord, turning itself right side out. Cut the covered cord into two 48-inch-long pieces.

17. Weave the fabric-covered cord straps through the grommets. Check the fit of the cords over your shoulder and trim to the desired length. Pull the fabric covering back to expose the cord; butt the ends and whipstitch together (Figure 9).

Figure 7
Add grommets.

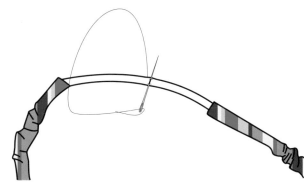

Figure 9
Whipstitch cord ends together.

13. With right sides together, fold the long bias strip in half lengthwise and stitch ¼ inch from the raw edges. Trim the seam allowance to ⅛ inch.

18. Slide the fabric back into place, turn under the raw edges and sew together. Slide the cords through the grommets so the "seam" is hidden on the inside of the bag. ●

TOILE TERRIFIC

DESIGN BY KAREN DILLON

To make this pretty tote, choose a decorator toile print and a solid coordinate for the lining. Pockets inside and out will make it a favorite for shopping and travel. Take extra care in cutting so the outer pocket matches up perfectly with the tote layer underneath.

FINISHED SIZE
12 x 9¾ x 6¼ inches, excluding straps

MATERIALS
• Approximately 1 yard 54-inch-wide toile print (decorator fabric); see Project Notes
• ⅞ yard 44/45-inch-wide coordinating solid-color cotton canvas or heavy linen for lining
• 1⅝ yards 22-inch-wide medium- to heavyweight fusible interfacing for bag
• 1⅝ yards 22-inch-wide light-weight fusible interfacing
• 2 (4 x 5-inch) rectangles of nonwoven synthetic suede or real leather for strap tabs
• ¼ yard lining for inner and outer pockets
• 4 (½ x 1-inch) rectangle rings for straps
• ⅞ x 10-inch piece grosgrain ribbon
• 1 small button
• 2 (¾ x 25-inch) strips polyester fleece for straps
• 4 x 5-inch piece paper-backed fusible web
• Pattern tracing paper or tissue
• All-purpose thread to match fabrics
• Rotary cutter, mat and ruler
• Basic sewing tools and equipment

INSTRUCTIONS

Project Notes: *Make the tote front/back pattern piece as directed in the first cutting direction and take to the store so you can check the size and positioning over the toile design to determine its suitability and the actual required yardage. Also cut one pocket rectangle and two side-panel rectangles from the paper. All seam allowances are ¼ inch wide.*

Cutting

• Enlarge the bag front/back pattern piece (Figure 1) on pattern tracing paper and cut out.

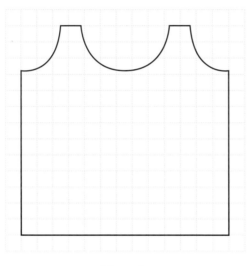

Figure 1
Tote Front/Back
1 square = 1"

• Center the pattern piece over a predominant pattern in the toile and cut out. Cut another piece for the opposite side of the bag, making the print placement identical to the first, if possible.
• Using the bag front as a guide, cut a 10½ x 13-inch pocket rectangle that will match the toile pattern when the lining is added and the pocket is attached to the bag panel.
• For the toile side panels, cut two 7 x 10¼-inch rectangles. Try to cut these so the pattern continues from the side panel to the bag front to the side panel when the seams are stitched.
• For the toile bottom panel, cut one 7 x 13-inch panel.
• From the heavier interfacing and the lighter interfacing, cut two bag front/back panels using the pattern piece. Also cut two 7 x 10¼-inch rectangles for the side panels and one 7 x 13-inch rectangle for the bag bottom panel.

• From the coordinating solid-color for the tote lining, cut two 2⅜ x 26-inch strips for the straps, two bag front/back panels, one 7 x 10-inch inner pocket rectangle and one 10½ x 13-inch inner pocket rectangle.
• From the pocket lining fabric, cut two 6½ x 13-inch rectangles.

Assembly

1. Following the manufacturer's directions, apply the heavier interfacing to the wrong side of all toile bag pieces and the lighter interfacing to the wrong side of the bag lining pieces.

2. Fold the ribbon in half crosswise and fuse the layers together with fusible web. Fold the ribbon in half lengthwise and stitch the short ends together in a scant ⅛-inch-wide seam. Press the seam open, and then turn the point right side out. Make a vertical buttonhole in the ribbon (Figure 2).

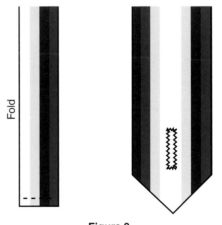

Fold

Figure 2
Prepare ribbon tab for closure.

3. Center the cut end of the ribbon face down at the upper edge of one of the toile bag front/back panels. Baste in place.

4. With right sides facing, sew the inner pocket and lining pieces together. Press the seam toward the lining. Fold with wrong sides together and raw edges even; press. Topstitch ⅛ inch from the upper edge. Repeat with the toile pocket and its lining piece (Figure 3 on page 14).

5. Position the toile pocket face up on the right side of the toile bag front/back panel without the ribbon tab. Baste the raw edges together. Repeat with the lining pocket and one bag panel.

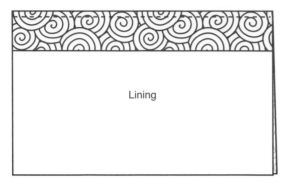

Figure 3
Prepare outer pocket.

6. To make the inside end pocket, fold the 7 x 10-inch solid-color panel in half crosswise with wrong sides facing and press. Edgestitch ⅛ inch from the upper edge. Pin to the right side of one 7 x 10¼-inch solid-color side panel and baste the raw edges together.

7. With right sides together, sew the solid-color side panels to the solid-color bag back, leaving the last ¼ inch unstitched at the bottom of each seam (Figure 4). Sew the remaining raw edges of the side panels to the coordinating solid-color bag front in the same manner. Sew the toile bag pieces together in the same manner.

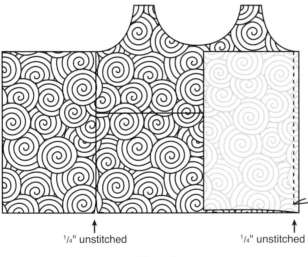

¼" unstitched   ¼" unstitched

Figure 4
Sew side panels to bag front and back panels.
(toile and contrast).

8. With right sides together, sew the solid-color bag bottom to the bag. The openings in the seam at the bottom of the bag will allow you to pivot neatly at the corners (Figure 5). Leave an 8-inch-long opening in one of the bottom seams for turning. Press the seams open. Repeat with the toile bag pieces; press the seams open and turn the bag right side out.

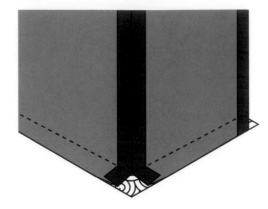

Figure 5
Sew bottom panel. Pivot at corners.

9. Tuck the toile bag into the solid-color lining and pin together with upper raw edges and seam lines matching. Stitch ¼ inch from all but the short upper edges of the strap extensions (Figure 6).

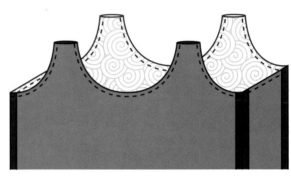

Figure 6
Sew lining to bag upper edge.

10. Turn the bag right side out through the opening in the lining. Turn under and press the lining opening edges and edgestitch together.

11. Tuck the lining into the bag and press the upper edge. Topstitch ⅛ inch from the pressed edge ¼.

12. Apply fusible web to the wrong side of one 4 x 5-inch suede rectangle; remove the backing paper and apply to the wrong side of the remaining rectangle following the manufacturer's directions and using a press cloth to protect the suede. Use rotary cutting tools to cut four strips, each 1 x 3½ inches and angle the ends as shown in Figure 7.

13. Wrap a suede tab over each handle ring and tuck the bag extensions between the layers. Topstitch (Figure 8).

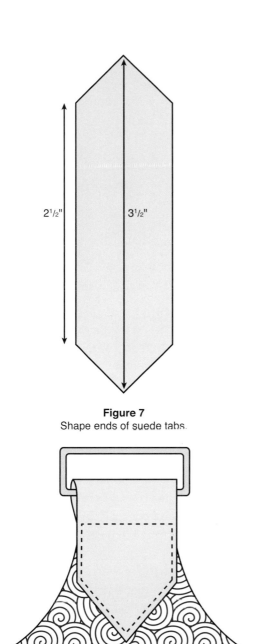

Figure 7
Shape ends of suede tabs.

2½" 3½"

14. To prepare each strap, position a strip of polyester fleece with one long edge even with long edge of a 2⅜ x 26-inch solid-color strap. There should be ½ inch of fabric extending beyond each end of the fleece. Stitch ⅛ inch from the raw edge. Machine-baste ⅜ inch from the remaining long edge of each strap.

15. Turn under and press the strap along the basting. Wrap the folded edge over the batting-backed half of the strap and press. Apply a narrow strip of fusible web to the turn under, and then turn the edge onto the back of the strip and fuse. On the right side of each strap, stitch ⅛ inch from each outer folded edge. Stitch through the center of the each strap, catching the folded edge on the underside (Figure 9).

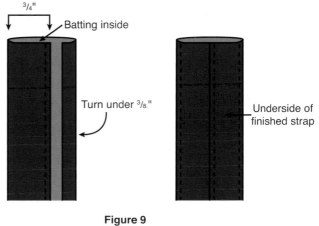

Figure 9
Prepare straps and topstitch.

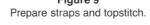

Figure 8
Attach tab and ring to bag extension.

16. Turn under and press ¼ inch at each end of each strap. Loop the ends of each strap through a set of rings on one side of the tote and pin in place 1 inch from the bar. Make sure both straps are the same finished length before stitching in place. Stitch again on top of the first stitching. ●

PICTURE THIS TOWN TOTE

DESIGN BY KAREN DILLON

Frame a pretty printed picture panel with ribbon on crisp pique for this oh-so-fresh and feminine bag. Button feet keep it clean on the bottom, and colorful cords show through hardware tubing for the clever handles.

FINISHED SIZE

10½ x 13¼ x 3¾ inches

MATERIALS

- One ink-jet computer-printed image measuring approximately 6 x 8 inches or 7 x 9 inches (see Note)
- ½ yard 44/45-inch-wide white cotton pique
- ½ yard firmly woven cotton for lining
- ¾ yard heavyweight nonwoven fusible interfacing
- 2 yards each of 5 different colors of rattail cord (colors from the printed image)
- 1 yard ⅝-inch-wide grosgrain ribbon
- 1 package mini piping
- Optional: small beads
- All-purpose thread to match fabric and ribbon
- Size 14/90 universal sewing machine needle
- Optional: 1 magnetic snap set
- 56-inch-long piece of clear plastic tubing (See Note)
- 36-inch-long piece of fine wire
- 4 (½-inch-diameter) buttons for bottom "feet"
- Bodkin
- Permanent fabric glue
- Rotary cutter, mat and ruler
- Basic sewing tools and equipment

Note: *Print the selected image on treated cotton poplin following the manufacturer's directions. If you prefer, you can substitute a pieced block, a preprinted fabric panel or a special piece of fabric for the computer-printed image. For panels that are smaller or larger than the suggested sizes, it may be necessary to adjust the cutting dimensions of the bag panels so that the frame around the image is equal.*

Do not purchase plastic tubing with printing on it, as it is not removable. If clear plastic tubing is not available, substitute ribbon, webbing or fabric straps, or straps made from matching fabric.

INSTRUCTIONS

Cutting

- Prepare the computer-printed image of your choice. For even more fun, make two prints, one for each side of the tote. You will need additional ribbon trim for this option.
- From the pique, cut two 11½ x 14-inch rectangles, two 5 x 14-inch side panels and one 5 x 11½-inch bottom panel. Cut the same pieces from the lining and from the interfacing.
- For the lining pocket, cut one 7½ x 13-inch rectangle.
- Apply the interfacing to the wrong side of each panel following the manufacturer's directions. **Note:** *For added firmness in the completed bag, cut and apply fusible interfacing to the lining pieces, too.*

Assembly

1. Trim excess fabric around the panel print, leaving a ⅜-inch-wide seam allowance beyond the image. Machine-baste ⅜ inch from the raw edges for a ribbon placement guide.

2. Center the panel on the right side of one bag rectangle and pin in place, or apply a light coat of temporary spray adhesive to the back of the panel and center on the rectangle.

3. Position the ribbon around the machine basting at the outer edge of the image as shown in Figure 1 on page 18 and edgestitch in place, mitering the corners as you go. Stitch the outer edge of the ribbon in place.

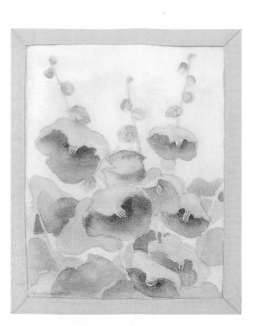

Figure 1
Center print on fabric.
Add ribbon and miter corners.

4. Optional: Outline some of the motifs in the print with stitching and add decorative beads as desired.

5. With a contrasting thread in the bobbin, position and stitch piping to the sides and bottom edges of each bag rectangle. The raw edge of the piping should be even with the raw edge of the fabric. Clip the piping seam allowance at the corner to allow you to turn the corners smoothly (Figure 2). Take care not to pull on the piping cord or the fabric as you stitch.

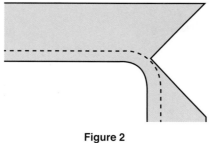

Figure 2
Clip piping seam allowance at corners.

6. Sew the side panels to the bottom panels, leaving ¼ inch unstitched at each end of each seam (Figure 3).

7. With right sides together, pin and sew the bag front to the side/bottom panel, pivoting at the corners. Stitch from the bag side (side panel against the machine) and use a zipper foot so you can stitch just inside the first piping stitching. Repeat with the bag back. Position a button on the bottom panel at each corner and sew securely in place.

8. Optional: If desired, cut and make pockets of the desired size and shape to apply to the lining before assembling the pieces and completing the bag.

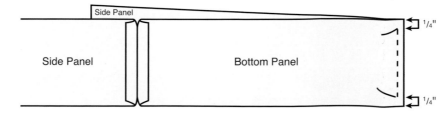

Figure 3
Stitch side and bottom panels together, leaving ¼" unstitched at ends of seams.

9. Prepare the side/bottom panel as you did for the tote and sew to the lining front and back panels, leaving an 8-inch opening in one of the bottom seams for turning.

10. Apply a 2½-inch square of fusible interfacing to the wrong side of the lining at the center of both upper edges to reinforce the snap closure—unless you have already applied interfacing to the lining for added body in the finished tote.

11. If desired, apply the snap closure to the lining right side with the upper edge of the closure at least 1¼ inches away from the upper raw edges of the lining.

12. Cut the clear plastic tubing into two equal lengths. At each cut end, cut away half of the tubing as shown in Figure 4.

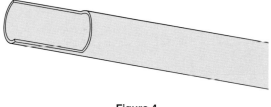

Figure 4
Cut away half of the tube at each end.

13. Cut each piece of rattail cord into two equal lengths. Group the cords in sets of five and tightly wrap one end of one set of cords with fine wire. Leaving the rest of the wire still attached, thread the end through a bodkin and push through the tube. Twist the cords inside the tube and stitch across the cord ends only (not the tubing) to secure the twists.

14. Position one handle on each side of the bag 1¼ inches from the side seams with the plastic tubing tab against the right side. Attach the zipper foot and adjust so the needle is to the left of the foot. Stitch back and

forth across the tubing and cord several times, taking care not to stitch on top of a previous row of stitching (Figure 5).

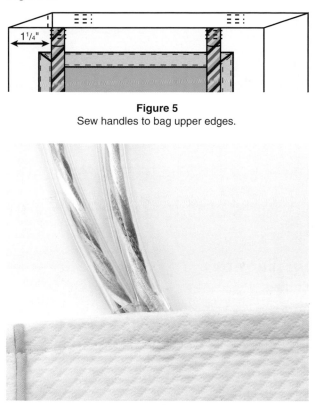

Figure 5
Sew handles to bag upper edges.

15. Tuck the tote with handles into the lining with seams matching and raw edges even. Stitch ¼ inch from the raw edges around the upper edge. Turn the tote right side out through the opening in the lining.

16. Turn under and press the seam allowances at the lining opening. Stitch the edges together. Tuck the lining into the bag and press the upper edge, taking care not to touch the tubing with the iron. Adjust the needle position to the right of the zipper foot and topstitch ½ inch from the upper edge of the tote. For ease, work over the free arm of the sewing machine. ●

TRIANGLES ALL AROUND

DESIGN BY JUDY MURRAH

Beaded appliqués add a little glitz to this colorful patchwork tote. Each side features a different block made from simple squares and triangles. Flirty fringe adds the finishing flourish.

INSTRUCTIONS

Cutting

• From the medium-value print, cut two 15 x 18-inch pieces for the lining. From the dark-value print, cut two 3½ x 30-inch strips for the handle. From the light-value print, cut two 5½ x 10-inch pieces for the pocket. Set these pieces aside for the bag assembly.

• From the light print, cut one 2 x 42-inch strip, one 2⅝-inch square and one 4¼-inch square. Cut the large square twice diagonally for four quarter-square triangles.

• From the medium-value print, cut two 3½ x 40-inch strips, two 2⅜-inch squares and two 4⅞-inch squares. Cut the squares in half once diagonally for four half-square triangles of each size.

• From the dark-value print, cut two 3⅞-inch squares. Cut once diagonally for a total of four half-square triangles.

• Set aside the pieces you have just cut (strips, triangles and squares) for Block A.

• From the remaining light print, cut two 8-inch squares for Block B. Cut each in half diagonally for four large triangles. Cut one 4¾-inch square and one 7¼-inch square. Cut the larger square twice diagonally for four quarter-square triangles.

• From the remaining medium-value print, cut two 3⅞-inch squares for Block B. Cut the squares once diagonally for four half-square triangles.

• From the remaining dark-value print, cut two 6⅞-inch squares for Block B. Cut the squares once diagonally for four quarter-square triangles. Set the pieces aside for Block B.

FINISHED SIZE

9 x 14 x 5 inches, excluding straps

MATERIALS

• ⅝ yard each of 3 coordinating cotton prints in a light, medium and dark value
• 2 (15 x 18-inch) pieces canvas
• 4 (¾ x 30-inch) strips fusible batting or fleece for handles
• Assorted sequin/beaded trims and appliqués
• Glue used for applying appliqués (such as Jones Tones All-Purpose Plexi Glue Dream Squeeze)
• All-purpose thread to match fabrics
• 1 yard fringe trim for upper edge
• 2 (5 x 9-inch) pieces of plastic canvas or sturdy template plastic
• Rotary cutter, mat and ruler
• Basic sewing tools and equipment

Assembly

1. Arrange the pieces as shown in the piecing diagram for Block A (Figure 1) and sew together in numerical order using ¼-inch-wide seams. Press all seams toward the triangles.

Figure 1
Block A
Add triangles to center square in rounds.

2. Measure the block through the center and cut two strips this length from the 2-inch-wide light strip. Sew to opposite sides of the block and press toward the strips. Add 2-inch-wide light strips to the remaining edges of the block in the same manner (Figure 2).

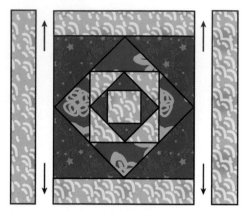

Figure 2
Add light strips to block.

3. Repeat step 2 to add 3½-inch-wide medium strips to the edges (Figure 3).

Figure 3
Add 3¹/₂" medium strips to block.

4. Trim the patchwork panel to 15 x 18 inches, making sure the block is centered so the strip widths are the same on each long side. The strips will be wider than the side strips at the short edges of the panel. Position the panel on a canvas panel and pin in place. Stitch in the ditch of the outermost seams to anchor the patchwork to the canvas. Machine-baste ¼ inch from all raw edges (Figure 4). Set the completed panel aside.

Figure 4
Baste block to canvas panel.

5. Position and glue (or stitch) appliqués in place as desired. Set the panel aside.

6. Referring to Figure 5, arrange the pieces for Block B and sew together in numerical order. Press all seams toward the triangles.

Figure 5
Block B
Add triangles to center square.

7. Fold the remaining piece of canvas in half with the long edges even and press to crease the center. Open the canvas panel and position the patchwork square on the canvas on point with the upper and lower points centered on the crease. The block will extend past the canvas at the long edges. Pin in place.

8. Add light triangles to the corners as shown in Figure 6. The oversize triangles will extend past the outer edges of the canvas. Flip the triangles onto the canvas and press. Trim the triangle edges even with the canvas. Machine-stitch ¼ inch from the raw edges.

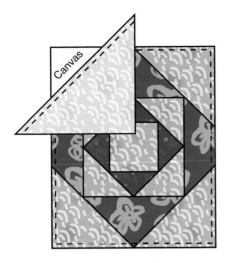

Figure 6
Add triangles to square on canvas panel.
Trim even with canvas edges and
baste ⅛" from outer edges.

9. Arrange appliqués as desired and glue (or stitch) to the panel.

10. With right sides facing, sew the pocket pieces together ¼ inch from all raw edges. Leave a 3-inch-long opening in one long edge (bottom) for turning. Clip the corners and turn right side out, turning the opening edges in. Position the pocket on one of the lining pieces as shown in Figure 7 and edgestitch in place, catching the turned opening edges in the stitching. Stitch through the pocket center to make a divided pocket if desired.

Figure 7
Stitch pocket to lining panel.

11. With right sides facing, pin the patchwork panels together. Cut a 2½-inch square from both layers at the bottom corners (Figure 8). Stitch ½ inch from the bottom raw edges and press the seam open. Topstitch ¼ inch from the seam line on both sides. Stitch the side seams and press open. Repeat with the lining pieces, leaving a 4-inch-long opening in the bottom seam for turning. *Do not topstitch the bottom seam.*

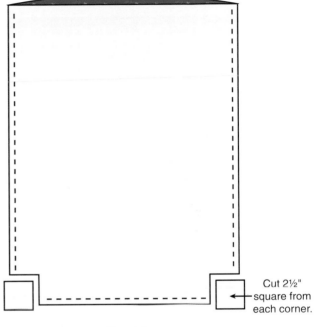

Cut 2½"
square from
each corner.

Figure 8
Stitch patchwork panels together.

12. With the side and bottom seam lines of the patchwork aligned, stitch ½ inch from the raw edges at each corner to box the bottom (Figure 9). Turn the bag right side out. Repeat with the lining, but do not turn the lining right side out.

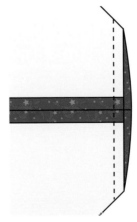

Figure 9
Align side and bottom seams; stitch.

13. Fold the strips for the handles in half lengthwise with wrong sides together and press. Open the strips and position two strips of fleece on the wrong side of each strip with edges meeting at the crease. Turn the long raw edges over the fleece strips and press (Figure 10). Fold the strip in half and topstitch ¼ inch from each long edge.

Figure 10
Position two batting strips along center crease.

14. Position the handles at the upper edge of the tote with the edges 2 inches from the side seams. Machine-baste a scant ½ inch from the raw edges.

15. Tuck the bag into the lining with right sides facing and pin together at the upper raw edge. Stitch ½ inch from the raw edge. Turn the bag right side out through the opening in the lining. Tuck the lining into the tote and press the upper edge. Edgestitch.

16. Position the fringe header at the upper edge of the bag, beginning and ending neatly at one side seam. Stitch close to both edges of the header.

17. Reach inside the opening in the bottom of the lining and place a dot of glue in several places on the tote bottom. Tuck the plastic canvas into the bottom of the tote through the lining and press it into the glue. Allow to dry.

18. Stitch the folded edges of the opening closed. Tuck the lining back into the tote. ●

OH! KIMONO!

**DESIGN BY
LINDA TURNER GRIEPENTROG**

This soft tote is the perfect place to showcase a collection of vintage kimono fabrics or some wonderful old ties. Make it in beautiful silk, rugged denim, suiting-weight linen, even synthetic suede.

INSTRUCTIONS

Project Notes: *Measurements include ¼-inch seam allowances unless otherwise stated. Cut the length of the tote pieces parallel to the selvages.*

Cutting

• From the bag fabric, cut two 7 x 18-inch rectangles for the bag front, one 18-inch square for the bag back and two 3½ x 24-inch strips for the handles.
• From the lining fabric, cut two 16 x 18-inch rectangles.
• From the kimono fabrics, cut 9-inch-long strips in assorted widths from 1½–2½ inches wide. You will need enough strips for a finished 18-inch-long band. Strip width variations add interest to the pieced band and allow you to cut around any stained or worn portions of the vintage fabric.
• From the quilt batting, cut two 18-inch squares.

Assembly

1. Arrange the kimono strips in the desired order and sew together using ¼-inch-wide seams. Press all seams in one direction.

2. Use rotary-cutting tools to trim the panel to 7 x 18 inches.

FINISHED SIZE

14½ x 14½ x 3 inches, excluding handles

MATERIALS

Yardages are for 44/45-inch-wide fabrics.

• ¾ yard silk dupioni for bag body
• ½ yard lining fabric
• ⅝ yard needled cotton quilt batting
• 2 (1¼ x 25-inch) strips of stiff interfacing, such as waistband interfacing, for the straps
• Assorted vintage kimono or tie fabrics for the patchwork, or substitute other fabrics of your choice
• All-purpose thread to match fabrics
• 1 (2-inch-long) Oriental charm
• 1 Chinese ball button
• 1 (3-inch-long) rayon tassel
• Temporary spray adhesive
• Air- or water-soluble marking pen
• Rotary cutter, mat and ruler
• Basic sewing tools and equipment

Insert the stiff interfacing into the strip and trim the excess interfacing even with the strap ends. Topstitch ¼ inch from each long edge.

6. Position one handle on the bag front with raw ends even and the inner edges at the seam lines for the pieced panel. Machine-baste a scant ¼ inch from the raw edges. Edgestitch the handle to the bag front for 2 inches, pivot and stitch across the handle and then pivot again and stitch the remaining edge to the bag front (Figure 2). Position the remaining handle on the bag back, matching the positioning on the bag front. Stitch as you did for the front straps.

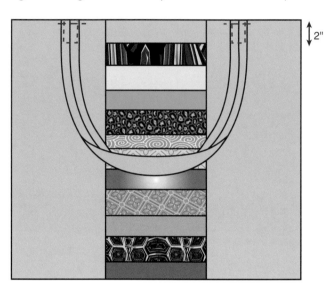

Figure 2
Baste handles to tote front and back. Edgestitch to hem allowance.

3. With right sides together, sew the 7 x 18-inch strips to the long edges of the kimono panel. Press the seams toward the pieced panel (Figure 1).

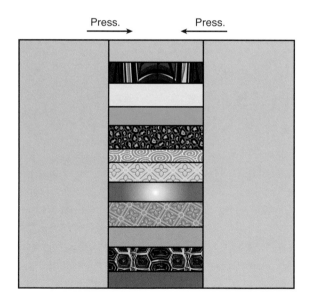

Figure 1
Sew pieced panel to side panels.

4. Apply a light coat of temporary spray adhesive to a piece of batting and smooth the bag front in place on top. Repeat for the bag back.

5. To make the bag handles, fold each 3½ x 24-inch silk strip in half and stitch the long edges together; turn right side out and press, centering the seam on the underside.

7. With right sides facing, sew the bag front to the back at the side and bottom edges. Press the seams open. Turn under and press a 2-inch-wide hem at the upper edge.

8. To box the bag bottom, align the side and bottom seam lines at each corner and pin. Draw a stitching line 1½ inches from the point. Stitch on the line and again ⅛ inch from the first stitching (Figure 3).

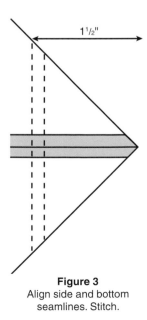

Figure 3
Align side and bottom seamlines. Stitch.

9. Trim the point close to the stitching. Do not turn the bag right side out.

10. With right sides facing, sew the lining pieces together along the side and lower edges, but leave an 8-inch-long opening for turning. Finish the bottom corners as shown for the bag. Turn the lining right side out.

11. Tuck the lining inside the bag with raw edges even. Stitch. Turn the tote right side out through the opening in the lining.

12. Turn under and press the lining opening edges and machine-stitch the turned edges together. Tuck the lining into the bag and re-press the upper edge of the tote. Optional: Topstitch ¼ inch from the upper finished edge.

13. Sew the button, charm and tassel to the tote front as desired. ●

Control Panels

If your kimono fabric is very lightweight or transparent, fuse tricot knit or lightweight weft-inserting interfacing to the underside before cutting into strips. This will prevent the seam allowances from showing through and give it comparable body to the other tote fabrics.

If you're using vintage ties for the pieced band, they're almost always cut on the bias, so it is essential to apply a lightweight nonwoven interfacing to the underside to control the stretch.

SEEING DOUBLE

DESIGN BY NANCY FIEDLER

This tote does double duty at the mall or at the beach. The clear carryall makes it easy to find your keys, and the hidden flexible frame snaps shut to keep everything securely inside. The pocketed portfolio has a handy wrist strap and holds items that you don't want the world to see.

FINISHED SIZE

12 x 13 x 4 inches

MATERIALS

- ⅝ yard 54-inch-wide clear vinyl
- ⅝ yard 44/45-inch-wide double-faced pre-quilted cotton print
- 4¼ yards 1-inch-wide nylon webbing or belting
- 4¼ yards 1-inch wide solid-color grosgrain ribbon
- 7 yards 1-inch-wide polka-dot or striped grosgrain ribbon
- All-purpose thread to match ribbon
- 14-inch zipper
- 18-inch Straight Hex-Open Frame (see Sewing Sources on page 175)
- Size 80/12 sewing machine needles
- Teflon presser foot for sewing machine
- Liquid seam sealant
- Rotary cutter, mat and ruler
- Pliers
- Basic sewing tools and equipment

INSTRUCTIONS

Project Note: *Use ½-inch-wide seam allowances throughout. Before sewing on the vinyl, read Smooth Stitching on page 31.*

Cutting

- From the vinyl, cut two 16½ x 21-inch rectangles.
- From the quilted cotton, cut one 15 x 25-inch rectangle, one 8½ x 10-inch pocket rectangle and one 9 x 7½-inch pocket rectangle.

Assembly

1. Sew the solid-color grosgrain ribbon to one side of the nylon webbing. Sew the polka-dot or striped ribbon to the opposite side of the webbing. There will be extra ribbon left for the upper-edge finish on the tote.

2. From the ribbon-covered webbing, cut two 64-inch-long pieces. Position on the vinyl rectangles as shown in Figure 1 and stitch in place along the edges.

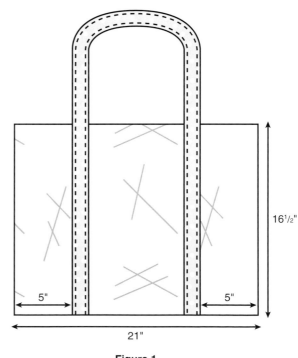

Figure 1
Sew straps to vinyl rectangles.

3. Cut two 18-inch-long pieces of the remaining polka-dot or striped grosgrain ribbon. Turn under and press ¼ inch at each end of each piece and stitch with a three-step zigzag stitch, if available on your machine. Otherwise use a short, narrow zigzag stitch.

4. Position the ribbon at the upper edge on the wrong side of each vinyl panel, centering it along the length of the upper edge. Stitch close to both long edges of the ribbon (Figure 2). Leave the short ends unstitched.

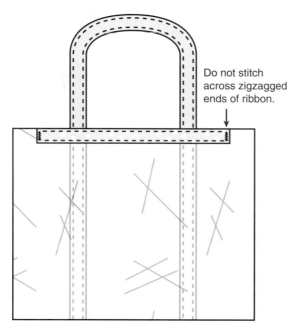

Do not stitch across zigzagged ends of ribbon.

Figure 2
Stitch ribbon casing to upper edge on vinyl wrong side.

5. From the remaining ribbon, cut two 21-inch-long pieces. Position a ribbon on the right side of the vinyl rectangles at the upper edge and stitch in place.

6. With right sides facing, sew the tote front and back together at the side seams. Finger-press the seams to one side and topstitch ¼ inch from the previous stitching through all layers.

7. With right sides facing, stitch the bottom seam and finger-press to one side. Topstitch ¼ inch from the seam line, if desired, to match the side seams.

8. Fold each corner with the side and bottom seam lines aligned and stitch 2 inches from the point to box the corners. Stitch again ⅛ inch from the first stitching (Figure 3).

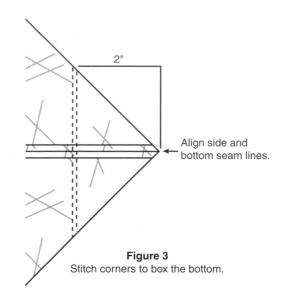

2"

Align side and bottom seam lines.

Figure 3
Stitch corners to box the bottom.

9. Turn the bag right side out and finger-press the bottom corner seams. Do not trim the triangle points.

10. Carefully insert the Hex-Open frame into the ribbon casing on the inside of the bag. Use pliers to hold the frame ends together to insert the rivets. Treat any exposed ribbon ends with seam sealant.

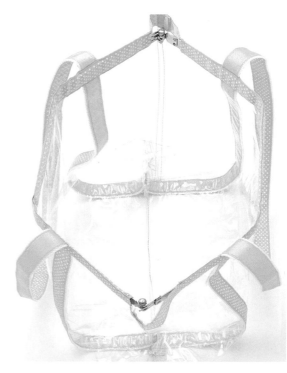

11. Use the contrast side of the double-faced pre-quilted fabric for the right side of the large pocket and the same side as the portfolio for the right side of the small pocket. Serge- or zigzag-finish all raw edges of each pocket rectangle. Turn under and press ½ inch at the upper edge of each pocket piece (a long edge). Topstitch in place. Repeat at the left edge of the smaller pocket piece

12. Position the small pocket on the large pocket with the raw edges aligned at the right and bottom edges. Topstitch the finished edge of the small pocket to the larger pocket and baste ¼ inch from the adjacent raw edges. Turn under and press ½ inch at all raw edges of the pocket.

13. Fold the bag rectangle in half and lightly press the bottom fold. Open the bag rectangle face up and position the pocket as shown in Figure 4. Topstitch in place. Cut an 18-inch-long piece of the remaining ribbon-covered webbing for the wrist loop and fold in half with raw ends even. Position at the upper edge of the bag front with the pockets and baste in place.

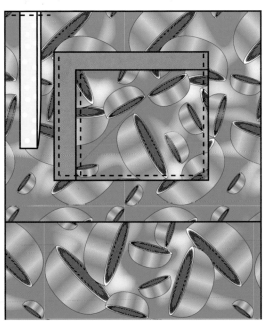

Figure 4
Sew pockets in place.

14. Sew the zipper to the upper edge of the rectangle, stitching ¼ inch from the zipper coil (Figure 5).

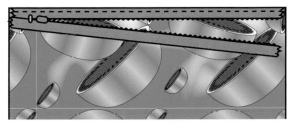

Figure 5
Sew zipper to upper edge of rectangle.

15. Sew the remaining half to the remaining upper edge of the portfolio in the same manner.

16. With right sides facing, sew the front and back together. Serge- or zigzag-finish the seam allowances together. Turn the portfolio right side out and tuck into the vinyl tote. ●

Smooth Stitching

Prevent vinyl from sticking to the machine and prevent pin damage while you sew.

• Use a Teflon presser foot to prevent the vinyl from sticking to the bottom of the foot while sewing on vinyl.
• Adjust the machine for slightly longer than normal stitch length (3mm) to prevent perforating the vinyl, which could cause it to tear at the seams.
• Use paper clips or binder clips instead of pins to hold the layers together for stitching.

CALIFORNIA DREAMIN'

DESIGN BY CAROL ZENTGRAF

A corded loop closure, flower button and shapely bamboo handles complete the carefree look of this breezy bag. Contrasting side panel inserts are a new twist on the traditional boxed bottom.

INSTRUCTIONS

Project Note: *Use ½-inch-wide seam allowances unless otherwise directed.*

Cutting

• Cut one 11 x 27-inch rectangle from the print and from the striped fabric. Cut one 11 x 27-inch rectangle from the fusible interfacing and apply to the wrong side of the print rectangle following the manufacturer's directions.

FINISHED SIZE

4 x 10 x 11 inches

MATERIALS

• ¾ yard 54-inch-wide floral print decorator fabric
• ¾ yard 54-inch-wide coordinating stripe decorator fabric
• ½ yard heavyweight fusible interfacing
• ½ yard ⅛-inch-diameter cotton filler cord for loop closure
• Bamboo purse handles (approximately 4½ x 7½ inches)
• 1½-inch-diameter decorative button
• All-purpose thread to match fabrics
• Rotary cutter, mat and ruler
• Basic sewing tools and equipment

• Draw two triangles (Figure 1) on the uncoated side of the fusible interfacing and cut out.
• On the wrong side of the striped fabric, align the center of each triangle with the center of a focal stripe and fuse to the fabric following manufacturer's directions. Cut out the triangles. Cut two additional triangles from the striped fabric. On the wrong side of all four triangles, mark the ½-inch seam lines at the lower corners and the point. Mark the center of each fused triangle base edge (Figure 2).

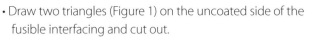

6½"

5½"

Figure 1
Draw 2 triangles on fusible interfacing.

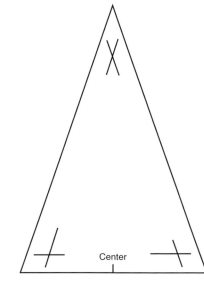

Center

Figure 2
Mark seam intersections and base center
on the wrong side of both triangles.

Assembly

1. On the right side of the print rectangle, mark the center of each long edge. Pin the triangles to the print fabric, aligning the center marks as shown in Figure 3. Stitch the triangle to the fabric, beginning and ending precisely ½ inch from each end of the triangle base.

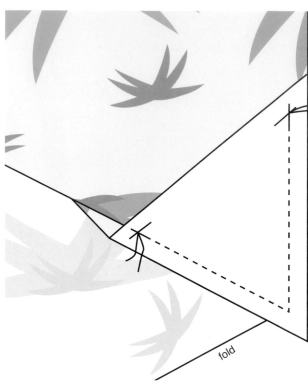

Figure 4
Sew side of triangle to bag edge.

3. Repeat with the remaining edge of the triangle. With right sides together, complete the bag side seam. Begin stitching at the point of the triangle and stitch to the raw edges at what will be the upper edge of the completed bag (Figure 5).

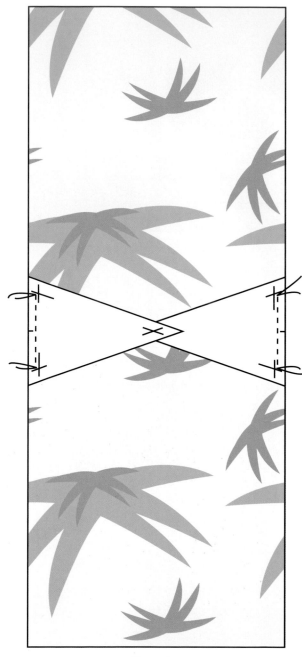

Figure 3
Stitch triangles to tote panel.

Figure 5
Sew second side of
triangle to tote panel.

2. Clip the print fabric edge to the stitching at each end and pin one remaining long edge of the triangle to the rectangle with raw edges even. Stitch, ending at the seam-line intersections at the point (Figure 4).

7. With the lining wrong side out, slip the bag inside, pin the upper edges together and stitch. Trim the seam allowance to ¼ inch. Turn the bag right side out through the opening in the lining side seam. Slipstitch or machine-stitch the opening closed. Turn the lining into the bag and press the upper edge, rolling the lining to the underside slightly. Topstitch ¼ inch from the upper finished edge

8. From the remaining striped fabric, cut one 1½ x 20-inch strip or two 1½ x 12-inch strips. Fold the strip(s) in half lengthwise with right sides together and stitch ¼ inch from the raw edges. Turn right side out and press with the seam centered in the tube. Cut five 3½-inch-long pieces for the handle loops and closure. At each end of each piece, turn the raw edges into the tube and edgestitch. Set one aside for step 10.

4. Repeat steps 2 and 3 to complete the remaining side seam. Assemble the striped lining in the same manner, leaving a 4-inch-long opening in the center of one side seam for turning.

5. From the remaining striped fabric, cut a 1½ x 13-inch bias strip. Wrap the fabric around the filler cord with right sides together and stitch ½ inch from the raw edges and across the cord. Trim the seam allowances to ¼ inch. To turn right side out, slide the tube over the excess cord. Cut across the stitched end of the fabric tube to trim away the excess cord, backstitching to secure (Figure 6a and b).

9. With the seam side up, position and stitch the strips to the bag front and back as shown in Figure 7. Fold each strip down to make a loop and stitch again as shown in Figure 7. Insert the handle ends through the loops.

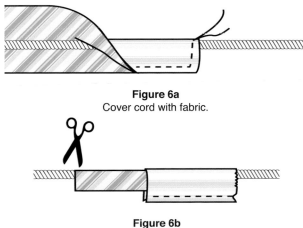

Figure 6a
Cover cord with fabric.

Figure 6b
Slide fabric back over excess cord.

6. Pin the cord ends to the center at the upper edge on the right side of the bag back. Machine-baste ⅜ inch from the raw edges.

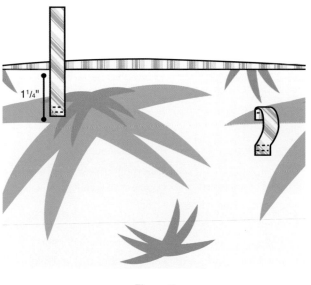

Figure 7
Sew loops to bag front.

10. To complete the closure, wrap the remaining 3½-inch piece of fabric around the loop, overlapping the strip ends in the center back. Stitch across the strip between the loop cords, being careful not to catch the covered cords in the stitching. Wrap the closure to the front of the bag and mark the button placement. Sew the button in place. ●

BEACHCOMBER TOTE

DESIGN BY LUCY B. GRAY

Little plastic "critters" abound in the toy bins at craft stores, and they make terrific embellishments for this nostalgic little tote crafted from a discarded cotton shirt—or new fabric if you prefer. Make the color-coordinated canvas lining before you begin the bag, following the directions for painting on a sand-washed color.

FINISHED SIZE
12 inches tall (excluding handle) x 7 inches wide (at base) x 3 inches deep

MATERIALS
Yardages listed are for 44/45-inch-wide fabrics.

- 1 rescued plaid cotton shirt or ¾ yard plaid cotton fabric in faded hues
- 14 x 24-inch piece of medium-weight cotton canvas to custom-color (see Note)
- ½ yard polyester fleece
- ¼ yard medium-weight fusible interfacing
- Pattern tracing paper or cloth
- 3 x 7-inch piece of plastic canvas for the bottom support
- Assorted small plastic beach critters
- 12 assorted-size buttons in coordinating colors
- Carpet thread (or buttonhole twist) in natural color
- Chenille needle
- Seam sealant
- Spray fabric protector
- Spray craft adhesive
- Industrial-strength craft glue
- Quick-drying craft glue
- Ruler
- Pencil
- Fine-tip permanent pen
- Rotary cutter, mat and ruler
- Basic sewing tools and equipment

Note: *Canvas lines the bag and adds support at the same time. If you prefer a more traditional lining, back the lining pieces with a firm fusible interfacing before sewing for added support and wearing durability.*

INSTRUCTIONS
Project Notes: *If you are using purchased fabrics, preshrink and press them before cutting. If you are recycling an old shirt, launder it first. Then cut all usable fabric free from the seams and press. Also preshrink the canvas.*

Cutting
- Before you begin cutting and constructing the bag, prepare the canvas with sand-washed color following the directions in Sand-Washed Color on page 41.
- Enlarge the pattern pieces (Figure 1 on page 38) on pattern tracing paper or cloth and cut out. Transfer the facing lines to the pattern piece. Place another piece of pattern tracing paper on top of the piece and trace off the facing pieces.
- From the plaid fabric, cut a front and a back outer bag piece, two facings, two bag handles and one pocket.
- Cut two 2 x 24-inch strips for the ruffles and two 1½ x 14-inch strips for the handle binding. Cut one 1½ x 6-inch strip for the pocket binding.
- From the polyester fleece, cut two outer bag pieces and one handle piece.
- Cut and apply fusible interfacing to the wrong side of each bag facing. You will cut the lining pieces from the custom-colored canvas later.

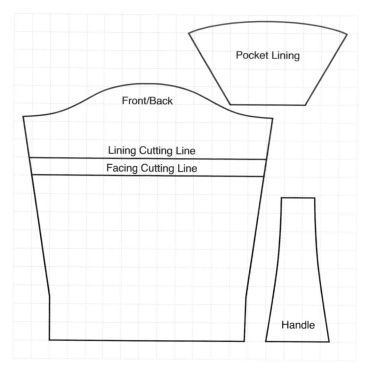

Figure 1
Beachcomber Tote Pattern Pieces
1 square = 1"

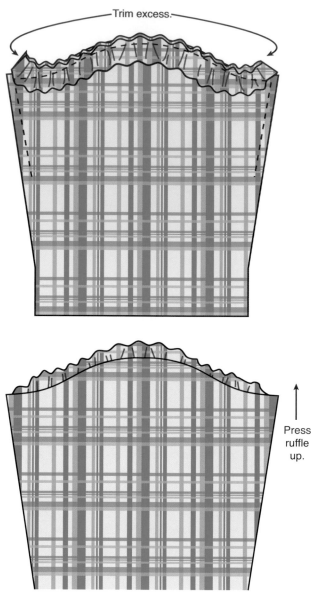

Figure 2
Stitch ruffles to bag upper edges.

Assembly

1. Apply a coat of craft adhesive to each piece of fleece and position on the wrong side of matching bag pieces and one handle piece. Smooth out any wrinkles. Lift the outer edges of the batting and trim away ³⁄₁₆ inch at the side and bottom edges of the bag front and back pieces. Weight the pieces with heavy books for 15 minutes to ensure a good bond.

2. Fold the ruffle strips in half lengthwise with wrong sides together and press. Machine-baste ⅝ and ⅜ inch from the raw edge of each strip. Draw up the bobbin threads to gather the strips to fit the upper edge of the bag (see Figure 2). Tie off the threads and then stitch over the gathers between the two rows of stitching.

3. Pin a ruffle to the upper edge of the bag front and back, angling the ends as shown in Figure 2. Stitch in place. Turn the ruffle up and press along the seam line. Remove the basting that shows in the ruffle.

4. Turn the ends of the ruffle down into the bag temporarily. Pin and stitch the outer bag pieces together at the sides and bottom edges, using a ¼-inch-wide seam allowance. Press the seams open.

5. To box the corners, align the side seamline with the bottom seam line and press. Draw a stitching line 1½ inches from the point. Stitch on the line, backstitching at both ends. Stitch again close to the first stitching and trim away the point (Figure 3). Turn the bag right side out and apply a coat of spray fabric protector following the directions on the can.

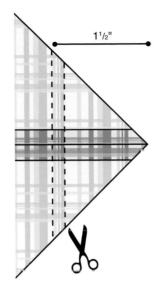

Figure 3
Stitch across point and trim.

6. With the fleece side of one handle against the wrong side of the remaining handle, pin the layers together. Machine-baste a scant ¼ inch from the raw edges. Pin and stitch a 1½ x 14-inch strip to each long edge of the strap using a ¼-inch-wide seam allowance. Press the strips toward the seams and wrap the remaining binding to the underside. Turn under the raw edge along the stitching and slipstitch in place with small stitches (Figure 4).

Figure 4
Bind both long edges of bag handle.

7. Apply a coat of fabric protector to both sides of the handle.

8. Center and pin the ends of the handle behind the ruffle on the bag front and back. Stitch in the ditch of the ruffle seam, backstitching at each end (Figure 5).

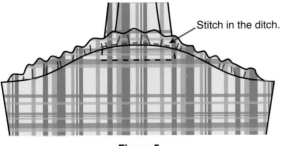

Stitch in the ditch.

Figure 5
Stitch handle to bag front and back.

9. Refer to the photo below. Cut two lining pieces from the painted canvas. With right sides together, pin the facings to the upper edges of the lining and stitch ¼ inch from the raw edge. Press the seams open.

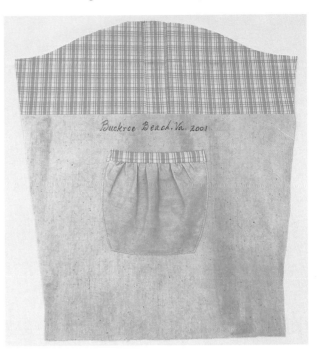

10. Stay-stitch ¼ inch from all edges of the pocket. Machine-baste on top of the staystitching at the upper curved edge; draw up the bobbin thread to gather the edge to 5 inches in length. Tie off the threads and machine-stitch on top of the basting to secure the gathers. Bind the gathered edge of the pocket with the 1¼ x 6-inch strip in the same manner as for the strap. Trim excess binding even with the pocket edges. **Note:** *If you prefer, you can cut a pocket from the painted canvas instead of the plaid.*

11. Turn under and press the pocket raw edges, using the staystitching as a guide. Center the pocket on the right side of one lining piece with the upper edge 2 inches below the facing seamline. Pin in place and edgestitch. If you wish to commemorate a special vacation trip, write the location and date above the pocket with a fine-tip permanent pen. Spray the lining pieces with fabric protector.

12. Trim ⅛ inch from the lower edges of the canvas lining. Repeat along the side edges, tapering to nothing by the time you reach the facing seamline. This makes the lining a bit smaller to fit smoothly inside your bag.

13. Pin the lining pieces together with right sides facing. Stitch ¼ inch from the side and bottom raw edges. Finger-press the seams open and box the corners as you did for the bag, but draw the stitching line 1⅜ inches from the corner instead of 1½ inches—to help the lining fit into the bag.

14. Place the plastic canvas in the bottom of the outer bag body. Use a dab of quick-drying craft glue at each corner to secure the canvas and allow the glue to set.

15. Insert the lining in the bag with wrong sides together and seam lines aligned. Turn under the upper edge of the lining along the ruffle stitching and pin in place. Slipstitch the turned lining edge to the ruffle.

16. Arrange plastic critters and buttons on the front of the bag as desired and mark their locations with pins. If you have a digital camera, take a picture for placement reference. Turn ordinary buttons into sea creatures with wavy "tentacles" by sewing the buttons on with multiple strands of color-coordinated carpet thread. (See step 8 of Sand-Washed Color on page 41.) First, thread a chenille needle with two 5-inch strands of dyed carpet thread. Then go through a button from the front, then through all bag layers, then back though the bag layers to the outside, and finally through the other buttonhole. Pull the threads even, cut the needle free, and tie the threads tightly with a single knot. Dab seam sealant on the knot. Trim the threads to different lengths and splay them in all directions, as though waves are moving the tentacles.

17. Use industrial-strength glue that is compatible with both a porous fabric and the nonporous surface of the plastic critters to glue them in place. Allow a full day for the glue to dry and harden. ●

Sand-Washed Color

You can create a custom-faded, sand-washed canvas for the bag lining and colored thread for the button tentacles following these easy steps.

SUPPLIES

- Acrylic paints in coordinating colors
- Disposable tray
- Paper towels
- Dish of water
- Large plastic trash bag
- Small resealable plastic bag
- Foam and artist's brushes
- Small pieces of sea sponge

1. Cover your worktable with a large plastic trash bag.

2. Place the canvas on the trash bag, wet it thoroughly, and smooth out any wrinkles.

3. Place blobs of acrylic paint the size of a quarter on a disposable tray and mix them slightly so that there are areas of both blended and pure color on the tray.

4. With a wet foam brush, begin streaking the damp canvas with the paint, adding water here and there to make the colors blend and dilute. Add more paint to your tray, as needed. You can paint stripes, polka dots, wavy lines, whatever inspires you!

5. When the entire canvas is covered, begin "scrubbing" the paint into the canvas with a wet sponge. This will smear and dilute much of what you've painted, but that's good.

6. Hang the canvas for a few hours where the paint drippings won't do harm.

7. Launder the canvas in cold water on a delicate cycle (without detergent), to remove any excess paint. Tumble the canvas in the dryer on high heat until completely dry. Press with a hot iron to remove wrinkles.

Note: *You may wish to run an empty load with detergent to remove any lingering paint from your washer.*

8. To custom-color the carpet thread used for the button tentacles, place a small amount of water in a resealable plastic bag. Add a single drop of acrylic paint in each of your chosen colors. Seal the bag and mix the colors. Add a small skein of carpet thread and reseal the bag. Wait several minutes to allow the color to soak into the thread, and then remove. Blot the thread with paper towels, and allow to air-dry. Using a protective press cloth, steam-press the thread skein to set the color.

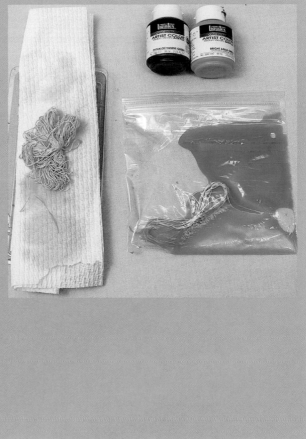

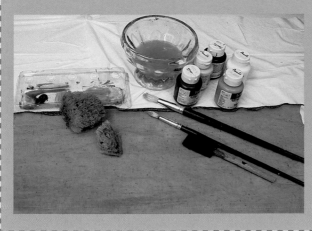

DENIM DELIGHT

DESIGN BY LINDA TURNER GRIEPENTROG

Denim is always a winner, no matter your age or lifestyle. This hobo-style bag holds all your everyday needs in casual comfort.

INSTRUCTIONS

Project Note: All seam allowances are ¼ inch wide, unless otherwise specified.

- Enlarge the bag pattern (Figure 1) on pattern tracing cloth.
- From the denim, cut two bag bodies, one 2½ x 15-inch strip for the straps and one 1 x 26-inch strip for the loops.
- Turn under and press ¾ inch at the upper edge of the bag body pattern piece and cut two bag bodies and one 6 x 6-inch square for the inside pocket from the lining fabric.
- From the interfacing, cut two bag bodies.

FINISHED SIZE

14½ x 14 inches

MATERIALS

- ½ yard 44/45-inch-wide denim for bag
- ½ yard 44/45-inch-wide cotton print for lining
- ½ yard medium-weight fusible interfacing
- 1 pair 23-inch-long flat braided leather handles with rings
- 1 child's leather belt (22 to 24 inches, buckled length)
- All-purpose thread to match denim and lining
- Light brown topstitching or jeans thread
- Size 80/14 denim or jeans sewing machine needle
- Chalk marker
- Pattern tracing paper
- Basic sewing tools and equipment

Assembly

1. Fuse the interfacing to the wrong side of the denim bag bodies following the manufacturer's directions.

2. Turn under and press ¼ inch on three sides of the lining pocket square. Turn under and press ¼ inch at the upper edge and then turn again and press for a double hem. Topstitch the hem in place.

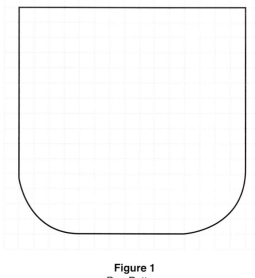

Figure 1
Bag Pattern
1 square = 1"

3. Center and pin the pocket to one bag body lining 6 inches from the upper edge; stitch in place along the side and bottom edges.

4. With right sides facing, sew the lining pieces together, leaving a 5-inch-long opening in the bottom seam for turning.

5. Turn under and press ¼ inch at each long edge of the 1-inch-wide denim strip for the belt loops. Fold in half lengthwise with the pressed edges even; stitch ⅛ inch from the long edges, using jeans thread in the size 80/14 needle. From the strip, cut nine 2½-inch-long belt loops.

6. Turn under and press ¼ inch at each end of each belt loop. On the bag front and back, draw a positioning line with the chalk marker 3½ inches from the upper raw edge. Position the loops on the bag body as shown in Figure 2. Topstitch in place at each short end. Use a short narrow zigzag stitch and backstitch at both ends.

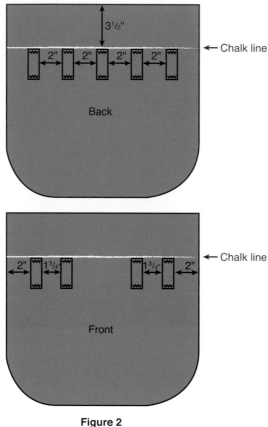

Figure 2
Sew loops to bag front and back.

7. For the strap loops, turn under and press ¼ inch at each long edge of the 2½ x 15-inch denim strip. Fold in half lengthwise with the pressed edges even; tuck a strip of fusible web between the layers and fuse. Stitch ⅛ inch from the long edges, using jeans thread in the size 80/14 needle. From the strip, cut four 2½ x 3½-inch pieces. Loop each piece through a metal loop of a braided strap and machine-baste the ends together ¼ inch from the raw edges.

8. Position the raw edges of the strap loops at the upper edge on the right side of the bag front and back 3½ inches from the sides (Figure 3). Take care not to twist the straps. Baste in place.

Figure 3
Baste straps to upper edge of bag front and bag back.

9. With right sides together, stitch the bag side and bottom seams, leaving an opening in the bottom edge for turning the bag right side out. Press the seams open, but do not turn the bag right side out.

10. Insert the lining into the bag with right sides facing and stitch the upper edges together. Make sure the strap loops are smooth and flat between the layers before stitching over them. Turn the bag right side out through the opening. Turn under and press the lining opening edges and edgestitch them together.

11. Tuck the lining into the bottom of the bag and press the upper edge. There should be a ¾-inch denim hem allowance. Topstitch ⅛ and ¼ inch from the upper edge, catching the strap loops in the stitching (Figure 4).

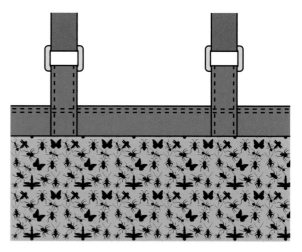

Figure 4
Topstitch upper edge, catching strap loops.

12. Thread the belt through the belt loops and buckle, pulling in the bag fullness as desired. ●

SLING TIME

DESIGN BY KAREN DILLON

Lightweight outerwear fabric is the perfect choice for this shaped and sporty shoulder bag. Consider other fabrics, including quilted cottons and home-dec coordinates, for a different look.

INSTRUCTIONS

Project Note: *All seam allowances are ¼ inch wide unless otherwise noted.*

Cutting

• Enlarge the pattern (Figure 1) for the flange on pattern tracing paper and cut out.

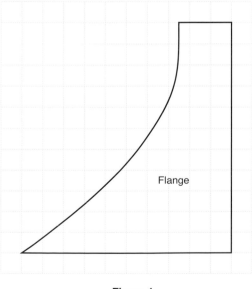

Figure 1
1 square = 1"

FINISHED SIZE

9 x 10½ (at bottom) x 2½ inches, excluding the shoulder strap

MATERIALS

• ½ yard lightweight 54-inch-wide sport fabric such as nylon Supplex, Cordura or pack cloth for the bag body
• ¼ yard for contrast and strap
• 1½ yards lightweight fusible interfacing (see Note at right before cutting the pieces)
• ½ yard lightweight cotton print for lining
• 14-inch sport zipper to match contrast fabric color
• All-purpose thread to match fabrics
• Pattern tracing paper
• Press cloth
• Basic sewing tools and equipment

Note: *Preshrink the fusible interfacing. If it is woven, knit or weft-insertion, dunk it in a sink of hot water and allow the water to cool. Squeeze out the water and allow to drip dry. If it is nonwoven, hold the iron soleplate ½ inch away from the interfacing and steam-shrink it.*

- From the fabric for the bag body, cut two 10½ x 13-inch rectangles. Fold the remaining fabric in half crosswise and use the pattern piece to cut two flanges.
- From the contrast fabric, cut two 3 x 13-inch rectangles and two 2½ x 35-inch straps.
- From the interfacing, cut two 10½ x 13-inch rectangles, two flanges and two 2½ x 35-inch straps.
- From the lining fabric, cut two 13-inch squares.

Assembly

1. Apply interfacing to the wrong side of all bag pieces using a press cloth and following the manufacturer's directions.

Note: If you did not preshrink the interfacing earlier, position the pieces on the wrong side of the bag pieces and steam with the iron without touching the interfacing before fusing.

2. With right sides facing, sew the short end of a strap to the short end of each flange. Press the seam open.

3. With right sides facing, sew the flange/strap units together at the long edges. Turn right side out and press with a press cloth to protect the fabric. Topstitch close to both long edges (Figure 2). Set aside.

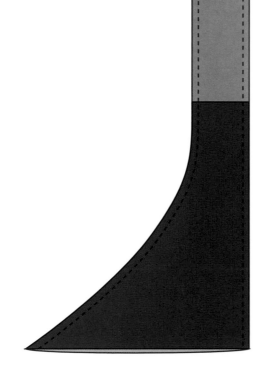

Figure 2
Sew flange to strap.

4. Shorten the sports zipper to 11½ inches by carefully removing the metal stop and repositioning it so the working length is 11½ inches. Cut off the excess zipper ½ inch below the new stop position.

5. Turn under and press ½ inch on one long edge of each 3 x 13-inch contrast rectangle. Place the folded edge of each strip ⅛ inch from the plastic zipper teeth and edgestitch in place (Figure 3).

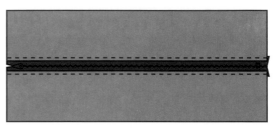

Figure 3
Stitch contrast panels to zipper (shown in contrasting color).

6. With right sides facing, sew the bag body pieces together along two sides and the bottom edge, leaving 2 inches of the side seams unstitched at the upper edges (Figure 4). Press the seams open.

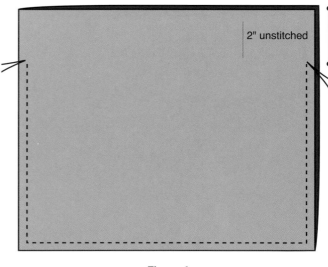

2" unstitched

Figure 4
Sew bag bodies together.

7. Box the bottom corners by folding each corner with the bottom and side seam lines aligned. Draw a stitching line 1¼ inches from the point. Stitch on the line and again ⅛ inch away (Figure 5). Trim the excess close to the second stitching.

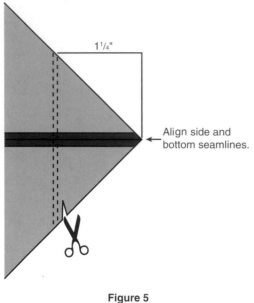

1¹/₄"

Align side and
bottom seamlines.

Figure 5
Stitch and trim corners to box the bottom.

8. Referring to Figure 6, pin the flange/strap unit to the upper edges of the bag back. Machine-baste a scant ¼ inch from the raw edges.

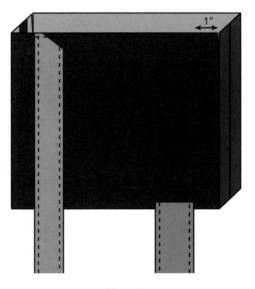

1"

Figure 6
Sew flange to upper edge of bag back.

9. *Unzip the zipper in the contrast panel.* With right sides facing, slip the contrast panel over the bag upper edges and pin in place with raw edges even. Stitch the flange to the bag front and back upper edges and press the seam toward the contrast. Edgestitch through all layers. Complete the bag side seams.

10. Sew the lining pieces together along the side and bottom edges. Press the seams open and box the bottom corners as shown for the bag in Figure 5.

11. At the upper edge of the lining, turn under and press ¾ inch. With wrong sides facing, slip the lining into the bag and slipstitch the upper edges to the zipper tape. From the right side, stitch again on the original zipper stitching.

12. With the zipper unzipped, stitch the bag to the flange from edge to edge, backstitching at the beginning and end of the stitching (Figure 7). ●

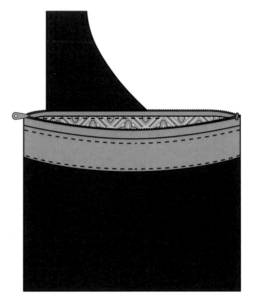

Figure 7
Stitch back edge of zipper to flange along edge of lining.

BEAUTIFUL BAGS

The stylish bags featured in the pages that follow are made from a variety of fabrics and trims. Try your hand at sewing with synthetic suede; make a shoulder bag from a scarf; embroider a piece of linen; try stamping on fabric for added embellishment.

BLACK & TAN & RED ALL OVER

DESIGN BY NANCY FIEDLER

Something as simple as natural-color linen becomes a spectacular accessory with the addition of decorative cords, machine embellishments, beads and buttons. Pull out the box of leftovers and look for inspiration among your treasures.

INSTRUCTIONS

Cutting

- From the red synthetic leather, cut two 2 x 16-inch strips for the frame casing and two 2½ x 24-inch strips for handles. Cut one 4½ x 16½-inch rectangle for the bag bottom.
- From the linen, cut two 9½ x 16½-inch rectangles for the bag front and back, and two 4½ x 10½-inch rectangles for the bag ends. Cut six 5-inch squares for the embellished appliqués.

FINISHED SIZE

8 x 16 x 4 inches

MATERIALS

- ½ yard 44/45-inch-wide red synthetic leather or suede fabric
- ½ yard 54-inch-wide natural-color heavyweight linen
- ½ yard 44/45-inch-wide woven cotton for lining
- 2 yards ½-inch-diameter cotton cord for handles
- 12-inch tubular purse frame (see Sewing Sources on page 175)
- 4 handbag "feet"
- ¼ yard heavyweight sew-in interfacing
- Assorted cords, ribbons and braids for decorative embellishments
- Miscellaneous beads and buttons
- Black decorative thread
- Black all-purpose thread
- Masking tape
- All-purpose threads to match fabrics
- Liquid seam sealant
- Ribbon/sequin foot to fit sewing machine
- Beading foot to fit sewing machine
- Size 14/80 needles
- Loop turner
- Pliers
- Basic sewing tools and equipment

- From the lining fabric, cut four 9½ x 16½-inch rectangles and one 4½ x 36-inch strip for the lining gusset.
- From the interfacing, cut one 4½ x 16½-inch strip.

Assembly

Project Note: *Use ¼-inch-wide seam allowances unless otherwise directed.*

1. Fold two of the lining rectangles in half lengthwise and press to create 4¾ x 16½-inch pocket panels. With side and bottom raw edges even, position and baste a pocket to the lower edge on the right side of each remaining lining rectangle. Machine-stitch from the top to bottom edge of each pocket panel to create divided pockets. Divide the pocket space evenly, or adjust the pocket sizing to fit specific items you carry in your handbag (Figure 1).

Figure 1
Sew folded lining panel to lining. Stitch.

Figure 3
Sew folded casing to bag front and back.

5. Fold one 2 x 16-inch casing strip in half with wrong sides together and long edges even; stitch to the upper edge of one bag piece. Fold and sew the remaining casing strip to the remaining bag piece in the same manner.

6. Fold each synthetic leather handle in half with right sides together and stitch ¼ inch from the long edges. Use the loop turner to turn the tubes right side out. If the ends of the cotton cord are not wrapped with masking tape, do so now. Sew a long length of heavy thread through one taped end of the cotton cord and pull the cord into one tube; trim cord so that 1 inch of the tube is empty at each end. Repeat with the remaining tube.

7. Sew the handles to the bag front and back at the marked positions (Figure 2). Cut four 1½-inch squares from the synthetic leather and sew a patch over the handle ends to hold them in place.

2. Fold one bag piece in half and draw around the edge of a coffee mug or small bowl to round off the lower corner. Pin the layers together and cut on the drawn line through both layers. Unpin and use the shaped piece as a pattern to shape the corners on the remaining linen bag and lining pieces (Figure 2). Mark the center at the bottom edge of each piece and the handle positions.

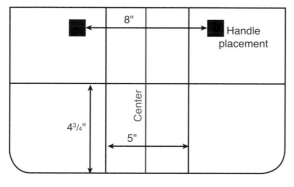

Figure 2
Bag Front and Back

3. Embellish each linen square with the desired decorative technique. See the bag photos for ideas, but don't feel you must copy these exactly. Refer to Decorative Techniques on page 54 for the stitching methods used to embellish the squares for this bag.

4. Refer to Figure 3 for steps 4 and 5. Arrange three embellished squares on the right side of the bag front and back pieces as desired. Topstitch in place ¼ inch from the raw edges. Fringe the edges of the appliqués by pulling out the crosswise threads up to the stitching line. Embellish the open spaces on the bag front and back as desired.

8. Position the interfacing on the wrong side of the 4½ x 16½-inch bag bottom panel. Machine-baste a scant ¼ inch from the raw edges. With right sides together, sew the bag ends to the bag bottom creating the bag gusset (Figure 4). Fold the gusset in half with short ends even and mark the center fold. Repeat with the lining gusset strip.

Center

Figure 4
Assemble bag gusset.

9. With centers matching, pin the bag gusset to the bag front panel. Beginning at the center, stitch the gusset to the bag and lock the stitches at the end. Sew the bag back to the remaining raw edge of the bag gusset (Figure 5). Press the linen portion of each seam toward the gusset. Do not touch the synthetic leather or suede

Figure 5
Sew gusset to bag front and back.

with an iron. Turn the bag right side out. Attach the purse feet to the bag bottom following the package directions.

10. Repeat step 9 to construct the lining, but leave a 6-inch-long opening in one of the bottom seams. Press the seam allowances toward the bag front and back.

11. With right sides facing, slip the bag inside the lining. Sew the layers together along the upper edge without catching the gusset seam allowances in the stitching. Lock off the stitches at each seam line (Figure 6). Trim the excess gusset fabric as needed. Turn the bag right side out through the opening in the lining. Turn under and press the seam allowances at the opening edges.

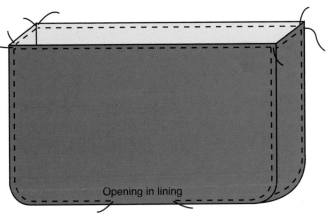

Opening in lining

Figure 6
Sew lining to bag at upper edge,
breaking the stitching at each gusset seam line.

12. Insert the tubular frame into the casings and push the rivets in place to form the hinges as shown in the package directions. Use pliers to hold the hinges together while inserting the rivets.

13. Stitch the turned edges of the lining opening together. Tuck the lining into the finished bag. ●

Decorative Techniques

Always test the technique and decorative stitches on a scrap of the desired fabric to determine the best settings for the desired effect. If the fabric puckers for any of the techniques, apply fusible knit interfacing to the wrong side of the fabric following the manufacturer's directions before you do the decorative work on the right side of the fabric.

Reverse Bobbin Work

1. Wind the bobbin with a heavy decorative thread. Place the bobbin in the bobbin case but bypass the tension. Thread the needle with matching-color all-purpose thread.

2. Select a decorative stitch; place the fabric wrong side up under the presser foot, lower and raise the needle one time and bring the bobbin thread to the top of the fabric, then start sewing.

3. When the stitching is complete, bring the bobbin thread to the wrong side of the fabric and tie the tails.

Couching

1. Place ribbon or braid in the guide of the ribbon/sequin foot, or place decorative cord in the guide of the beading foot.

2. Thread the machine in a color to match the trim. Set the machine for a zigzag stitch that is the same width as the trim.

3. Sew the trim in place, starting and stopping ¼ inch from the edges.

4. To secure the ends, place a drop of seam sealant at the ends of the braid or ribbon. When using a cord, leave a 2-inch-long tail at the beginning and end. After couching the cord, tie a knot at each cord end, trim excess cord and treat the cut end with liquid seam sealant.

Machine Embroidery

1. Place a piece of tear-away stabilizer in the appropriate-size embroidery hoop for the machine and the selected embroidery design.

2. Spray the back of the appliqué fabric with temporary spray adhesive and adhere the square, face up, in the center of the hoop.

3. Embroider the design, clip threads, unhoop and remove the stabilizer.

Decorative Stitching

1. Select a favorite built-in decorative stitch and thread the machine with embroidery thread.

2. Embellish the square in straight lines or random curves, starting and stopping ¼ inch from the raw edges.

Bead & Button Embellishments

After the appliqués have been sewn to the bag, sew on beads and/or buttons as desired.

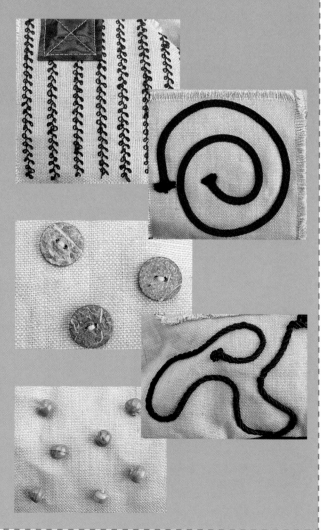

FLOWER POWER

DESIGN BY CAROL ZENTGRAF

Here's a breezy bag that's so easy to sew you'll want to make several to coordinate with your favorite wardrobe pieces. Home dec fabrics offer great coordinates for the outer fabric and lining, but feel free to dress this bag up in quilted velvets, or try it in denim with a red drawstring for a more casual approach.

INSTRUCTIONS

Project Note: *All seam allowances are ½ inch wide.*

Cutting

• Cut one 5 x 14-inch bag bottom and two 9½ x 18-inch bag bodies from the floral print and from the plaid fabric for the lining. Repeat with the interfacing.
• Following the manufacturer's directions, fuse the interfacing to the wrong side of the floral rectangles.

Assembly

1. Staystitch a scant ½ inch from the lower edge of each large floral rectangle to reinforce the seam. Fold each piece in half crosswise and mark the center fold at the upper and lower edges. Fold the 5 x 14-inch floral strip in half cross-wise and mark the center fold at both long raw edges. Fold in half lengthwise and mark the center at each short end.

FINISHED SIZE

13 x 8 x 4 inches

MATERIALS

• ⅓ yard floral print (home dec fabric; see Note at right)
• ⅓ yard plaid (home dec fabric)
• ⅜ yard nonwoven synthetic suede
• ⅓ yard 22-inch-wide heavy-weight fusible interfacing
• 3 yards ¼-inch-diameter cotton filler cord
• 4 x 13-inch rectangle plastic needlepoint canvas for bottom support
• Temporary spray adhesive (optional)
• Air-soluble marking pen
• Permanent fabric adhesive
• Small, sharp scissors
• 14 gold grommets
• Grommet pliers
• All-purpose thread to match fabrics
• Basic sewing tools and equipment

Note: Home dec fabrics are heavier and have usually been treated for stain resistance, so they make great fabrics for handbags. If you choose other fabrics with less body, you can easily add support and weight by applying a fusible interfacing to the wrong side of the bag and lining pieces before you begin the construction.

2. With right sides facing, sew the short ends of the large floral rectangles together. Press the seams open (Figure 1).

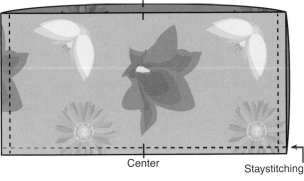

Figure 1
Sew shorts ends (not bottom edges) together.

3. With the centers of the short ends matching the side seams, and the center front and center back marks matching, pin the bag bottom to the bag front and back. Clip the bag to the staystitching at the corners as shown in Figure 2 so you can pivot and stitch smooth, square corners. Turn right side out and press.

Figure 2
Sew bag bottom to bag body.

4. Apply fabric adhesive around the inside bottom edges of the floral bag and put the needlepoint canvas panel in the bottom. Press it into the glue with your fingers and allow the glue to dry thoroughly.

5. Construct the lining from the plaid fabric following steps 1–3, but leave a 10-inch opening in one of the bottom long edges for turning. *Do not turn right side out.*

6. With right sides facing, place the floral bag inside the lining and stitch together around the upper edge. Trim the seam allowance to ¼ inch and carefully turn the bag right side out through the opening in the lining. Turn

under and press the lining opening edges; edgestitch together. Tuck the lining into the bag and press the upper edge. Topstitch ¼ inch from the upper edge.

7. Mark placement circles for three pairs of grommets on the bag front and back as shown in Figure 3. Mark a grommet placement circle over each side seam line, for a total of 14 grommets all around (Figure 3).

Figure 3
Apply grommets to front and backs edges of bag.

8. Use the small, sharp scissors to cut small holes for the grommets. Follow the directions with grommet pliers to attach the grommets, placing the washers on the inside of the bag.

9. From the faux suede, cut enough 1½-inch-wide straight-grain strips to make a 108-inch-long strip. Sew the pieces together by overlapping the short ends and topstitching.

10. ***Optional:*** *Apply a light coat of temporary spray adhesive to the wrong side of the suede strip.* Center the cotton filler cord on the wrong side of the strip and wrap the suede around the cord with the raw edges even. Attach the zipper foot and adjust the needle to the right of the foot. Stitch close to the cord and then trim the seam allowance close to the stitching.

11. For the drawstring, cut a 36-inch-long piece from the suede-covered cord. Beginning at one center front grommet, weave the cord in and out of the grommets around the bag. Knot the ends, adjust the cord as desired and tie in a knot.

12. Thread the remaining suede-covered cord through the side grommets. Knot each cord end and then tie the cords together in an overhand knot 1½ inches from the ends. Position the knot at one side of the bag and adjust the straps to create a double handle ●

ROLL OUT THE BARREL

DESIGN BY CAROL ZENTGRAF

This so-soft faux suede barrel bag features a stamped-and-pieced body with buckle-on handles. Stamping on fabric with textile paint is fun and easy when you use clear stamps so you can see the design positioning as you work.

INSTRUCTIONS

Project Note: *Use ½-inch-wide seam allowances.*

Cutting

- From the tan suede, cut one 5 x 19-inch strip for the bag center, two 5⅝-inch-diameter circles for the ends and two 1½ x 21-inch strips for the piping.
- From the pink suede, cut one 3 x 19-inch strip for the bag body and two 2 x 25-inch strips for the straps.
- From the purple suede, cut one 3 x 19-inch strip for

FINISHED SIZE

5 x 5 x 12 inches

MATERIALS

- ⅓ yard tan synthetic suede
- ¼ yard pink synthetic suede
- 3 x 22-inch strip purple synthetic suede
- 3 x 27-inch strip turquoise synthetic suede
- 3 x 19-inch strip yellow synthetic suede
- ⅝ yard 44/45-inch-wide lining fabric
- All-purpose thread to match fabrics
- 1¼ yards cotton filler cord for piping
- 1 yard of fusible structural stabilizer (see Sewing Sources on page 175)
- 4 (1⅛-inch-wide) metal buckles
- 1 magnetic snap set
- 2 yards 1¼-inch-wide stiff waistband interfacing
- Optional: Clear stamp, textile paint and stamp pad
- Narrow basting tape
- Awl
- Rotary cutter, mat and ruler
- Press cloth
- Basic sewing tools and supplies

the bag body and four 1 x 1½-inch strips for the buckle attachments.
- From the lining fabric, cut one 13 x 17-inch rectangle and two 5⅝-inch-diameter circles.
- From the structural stabilizer, cut three 11 x 19-inch rectangles and six 4⅝-inch-diameter circles.

Assembly

1. For the optional stamping on the tan suede panel, refer to Stamping Fabric on page 61. If desired, you can leave this panel plain, or add machine-embroidered motifs in place of the stamping. If you prefer to stamp the fabric, it is essential to allow the paint to dry overnight before proceeding with the bag construction.

2. Referring to the photo, arrange the suede strips in order and sew the long edges together using ½-inch-wide seams. Finger-press the seams open or press open with the tip of an iron, protecting the suede with a press cloth.

3. Following the manufacturer's directions, center and fuse the structural stabilizer to the wrong side of the pieced panel. Fuse the remaining rectangles in place on top of the first rectangle, taking care to keep the raw edges of the stabilizer even all the way around.

4. From the stiff waistband interfacing, cut two 12-inch-long pieces. Center one piece along one 13-inch-long

edge on the wrong side of the pieced panel. Stitch in place ¼ inch from the edge (Figure 1a). On the right side, center half of the magnetic snap ½ inch from the fabric edge. Make two small slits through the suede and the waistband interfacing and insert the prongs of the snap. Bend the prongs away from the center to secure. Turn under along the waistband interfacing edge and topstitch in place (Figure 1b).

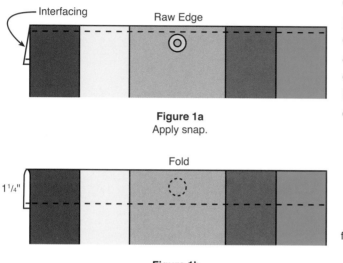

Figure 1a
Apply snap.

Figure 1b
Turn raw edge to inside along interfacing. Topstitch.

5. Draw a placement line ¼ inch from one long edge of the remaining piece of waistband interfacing. With the pieced panel face up, position the raw edge at the line on the interfacing. Pin in place and zigzag the panel to the interfacing (Figure 2a). Turn the interfacing to the wrong side of the panel and topstitch the edge in place. Lap the edge with the snap on the turned edge by 1¼ inches and mark the placement for the remaining snap half. Attach the snap at the mark as directed for the first half of the snap (Figure 2b). Snap the finished edges together and secure at the outer raw edges with small pieces of basting tape (Figure 2b).

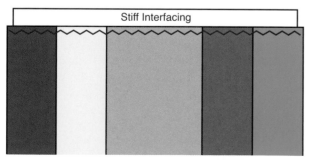

Figure 2a
Lap raw edge onto interfacing and zigzag in place.

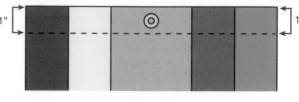

Figure 2b
Turn interfacing to wrong side. Apply socket half of snap.

6. Refer to Figure 3 for steps 6 and 7. To mark the placement for each buckle, measure 3½ inches from the closed edge and make a mark in the center of the yellow and pink suede strips on both halves of the panel. Wrap each 1 x 1½-inch purple strip around the lower bar of a buckle, and with raw edges even, stitch each one in place on the suede panel.

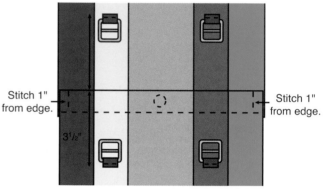

Figure 3
Sew buckles to bag panel. Stitch overlaps together.

7. Overlap and snap the finished pieced panel edges together again. Machine-stitch through all layers 1 inch from the raw edges to secure the overlap.

8. To make the piping, cut two 21-inch-long pieces of cotton cord. Wrap each piece with a 1½ x 21-inch strip of tan suede with wrong sides together and raw edges even. Machine-baste close to the cord, using a zipper foot adjusted to the right of the needle. Or, use a welting or piping foot if you have one for your machine.

9. Apply the piping to each end, beginning at the center of the panel opposite from the snapped edge. Use basting tape to apply the piping to the edge with the raw edges even and the piping cord toward the center. Baste in place along the piping basting line. To join the piping ends, remove several basting stitches from one end and open the fabric to expose the cord. Cut the cord even with the beginning end and re-cover the cord as shown in (Figure 4). Stitch in place close to the cord.

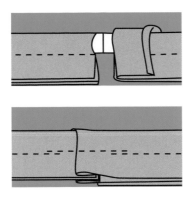

Figure 4
Join piping ends.

10. Layer and fuse three structural stabilizer circles to the center on the wrong side of each 5⅝-inch suede circle. Turn the bag wrong side out. With right sides together, pin and stitch a circle to each end of the bag.

11. On each lining circle, turn under and press ½ inch around the outer edge. Apply permanent fabric adhesive to the underside of each circle around the outer edge and glue in place on the inside of the bag to cover the structural stabilizer.

12. Turn under and press ½ inch at all four edges of the lining rectangle. Position over the stabilizer on the inside of the bag and slipstitch the turned edges in place. If you prefer, glue the lining in place and allow to dry. Turn the bag right side out.

13. For the straps, cut two 21-inch-long pieces of waistband interfacing and trim each one to ¾ inch wide. Wrap each strip with a 21-inch-long strip of pink suede, having the wrong sides together and raw edges even. Topstitch both long edges. Use an awl or stiletto to make holes in the strap ends for the buckle prong. Buckle in place and tuck the strap ends to the underside of the buckles. ●

Stamping Fabric

It's especially easy to stamp fabric with a clear acrylic stamping block. Textile paint remains soft while offering good coverage. To stamp the fabric, follow these easy steps. Test first on fabric scraps.

1. Pour a small amount of textile paint onto a stamp pad. Use the back of a spoon to work it in until the pad is saturated.

2. Lightly tap the stamp up and down on the pad until the image is covered, but not saturated. Hold the stamp by the edges and press it straight down on the fabric, pushing the stamp evenly with the fingers of your other hand. Lift the stamp straight up.

3. Repeat to stamp as many images as desired, cleaning the stamp if paint begins to accumulate in the cutout areas. Clean the stamp with mild soap and a toothbrush immediately after use.

4. Allow the paint to dry overnight or until thoroughly dry. Heat-set by pressing each image for 30–45 seconds with the hottest setting the fabric will tolerate. Use a press cloth to protect the synthetic suede and other fabrics that cannot withstand the heat of the iron.

PLAID SHE SAID!

DESIGN BY BARBARA WEILAND

Add a little bit of suede, too. Sew this roomy cloth bag from a wonderful wool plaid and accent it with faux suede details. Pockets inside keep valuables safe in this classy, lined bag.

FINISHED SIZE

17 x 11½ x 3 inches

MATERIALS

- 1 yard 54-inch-wide plaid wool
- ⅝ yard 44/45-inch-wide cotton canvas for inner support
- ⅝ yard 45-inch-wide synthetic suede
- ⅔ yard lining fabric for bag
- ¼ yard lining fabric to match suede for carriers.
- 1 yard 22-inch-wide weft-insertion fusible interfacing
- 9-inch invisible zipper to match lining
- 12-inch-long piece of trim or rickrack for inside zipped pocket
- 2 yards ⅜-inch-wide elastic for strap reinforcement
- Pattern tracing paper
- Air-soluble marking pen
- Dressmaker's chalk
- Size 90 universal needle
- ½-inch-wide strips of fusible web
- All-purpose thread to match fabrics
- Invisible zipper foot for your machine
- Press cloth
- Point turner for pressing
- Rotary cutter, mat and ruler
- Bodkin or large safety pin
- Basic sewing tools and equipment

Note: *Check your fabric and notions collection for fabrics for this bag. Every item used in this bag came from the designer's stash. She had hoarded the plaid wool for over 30 years! Lining scraps, zipper, elastic, canvas—it was all "free." The results—a beautiful designer bag to rival similar styles that sell for $500 and up.*

INSTRUCTIONS

Project Note: *Use ½-inch-wide seam allowances unless otherwise directed.*

Cutting

- On pattern tracing paper, draw an 18 x 30-inch rectangle for the bag body pattern, and draw grainlines on the vertical straight of grain for the interfacing and on the true bias for the bag body (Figure1 on page 64). Cut out the pattern piece.
- Position the bag body pattern piece on a single layer of the wool with the true-bias line aligned with the straight of grain so the bag body will be on the bias. Cut a matching piece from interfacing, but place the straight grainline parallel with the straight grain in the interfacing. Fuse the interfacing to the wrong side of the bag body following the manufacturer's directions. Make sure the interfacing is securely fused. By cutting the interfacing on the straight grain and fusing it to the bias-cut bag body, you stabilize the wool and prevent stretching during use.
- From the canvas for the inner support, cut one 18 x 26¾-inch rectangle on the straight of grain.
- From the lining fabric, cut two 13 x 18-inch rectangles for the bag lining, one 6 x 11-inch rectangle for the divided inside pocket and one 8 x 12-inch rectangle for the inside zipped pocket. Cut matching pieces of

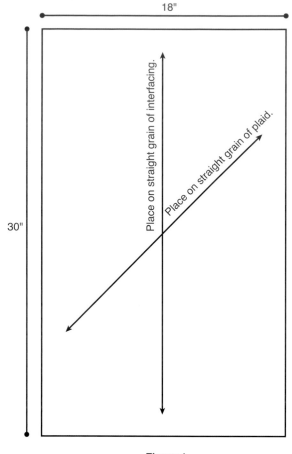

Figure 1
Make bag pattern.

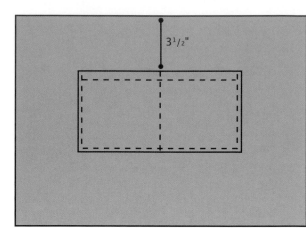

Figure 2
Sew pocket to lining panel.

2. Center and apply one half of the invisible zipper to one long edge of the 8 x 12-inch pocket rectangle. Turn the zipper tape to the inside and press. Slipstitch the lower end of the folded edge of the pocket to the zipper tape in the section you could not stitch above the zipper stop. Position the trim or rickrack in the center of the remaining zipper tape, turning the ends over the ends of the zipper tape ends. Stitch in place (Figure 3). Turn under and press the excess pocket at each end of the zipper. Turn under and press ½ inch at the lower edge of the pocket

fusible interfacing for the two pocket rectangles, and fuse to the wrong side of each piece following the manufacturer's directions.

- From the synthetic suede, cut two strips each 1¾ x 30 inches for the straps and set aside. From the remaining synthetic suede, cut one 7½ x 18-inch strip for the bag bottom panel and two strips each 6½ x 11½ inches for the strap carriers. From the fusible interfacing, cut pieces to match the rectangles. Apply to the wrong side of each piece following the manufacturer's directions.

Assembly

1. Turn under and press ½ inch on all four edges of the 6 x 11-inch lining pocket rectangle. At one long edge, turn under and press an additional ½ inch and stitch close to the inner edge to complete the upper-edge hem. Fold the pocket in half crosswise and lightly press the fold to mark the center stitching line. Position the pocket on the right side of one of the 13 x 18-inch lining rectangles and stitch in place (Figure 2).

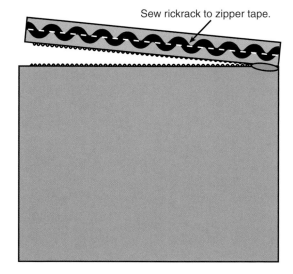

Figure 3
Sew half of invisible zipper to upper edge of pocket.

3. Position the pocket on the remaining lining rectangle and stitch in place along the pocket edges and through the center of the rickrack (Figure 4).

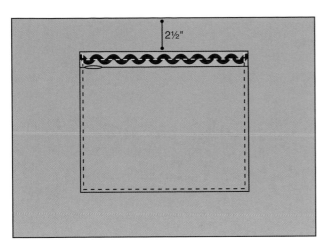

Figure 4
Stitch through center of rickrack and along pocket edges.

4. With the lining pockets facing each other, sew the two lining pieces together along the short ends and across the bottom; leave an 8-inch-long opening in the bottom seam for turning. Press the seams open over the point turner.

5. To box the bottom corners, fold the lining with side and bottom seam lines aligned and pin. Draw a stitching line across the point and stitch. Stitch again ¼ inch from the first stitching (Figure 5). Trim the excess point close to the second row of stitching. Do not turn the lining right side out. Set aside.

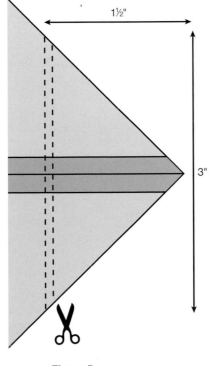

Figure 5
Stitch across corners and trim.

6. Fold the canvas rectangle in half crosswise and stitch the side seams. Press the seams open and box the bottom corners as shown for the bag lining. Set aside.

7. Fold the wool for the bag in half crosswise and snip the fold at each side to mark the placement for the bottom panel. Fold the 7½ x 18-inch suede rectangle in half lengthwise and snip-mark the fold at each end.

8. Center the suede right side up on the bag panel and fuse in place with narrow strips of fusible web tucked under the long edges. Use a press cloth to protect the suede. Edgestitch in place at each long edge (Figure 6).

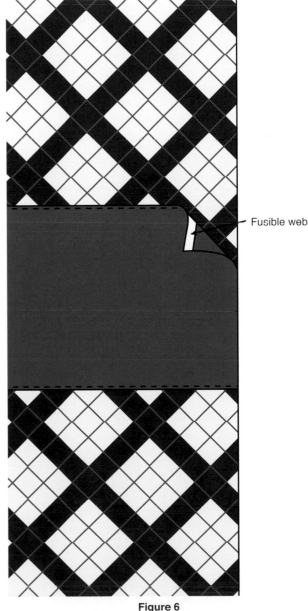

Fusible web

Figure 6
Fuse and then stitch suede to bag panel.

9. Use dressmaker's chalk to mark a grid for quilting the bottom panel to the bag. Space the lines approximately 1½–2 inches apart, depending on the plaid design. Align the chalked lines with lines in the plaid. Stitch on the marked lines, backstitching at the beginning and end of each row. Pull threads to the inside and clip.

10. With right sides together, stitch the lining to each 6½ x 11½-inch suede rectangle. Stitch ¼ inch from the raw edges and leave one long edge unstitched. Clip the corners, turn right side out and press, using a press cloth to protect the fabrics.

Note: To make it easier to turn and press the lining, understitch the seams. Begin and end the understitching as close to the corners as possible.

Machine-baste the raw edges together. Position a carrier at each end of the bag panel and edgestitch in place (Figure 7).

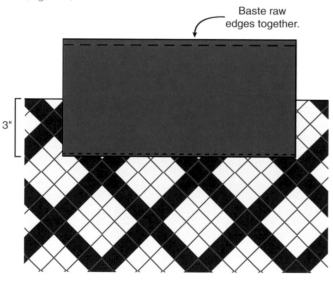

Baste raw edges together.

3"

Figure 7
Edgestitch carriers to ends of bag panel.

11. Fold the bag panel in half with right sides facing and the suede edges even at the side seams. Pin securely. Before you stitch permanently, machine-baste the lower end of each side seam, beginning and ending the stitching 1 inch above and below the suede edges. Check the basted seams to make sure the suede edges are aligned for a perfect match on the outside of the bag. If not, adjust the seams and check again before stitching permanently. Press the seams open and box the bottom corners as you did for the lining and the

canvas insert. Use a size 90 universal needle in the sewing machine to handle the heavy layers in the bottom. Stitch slowly. Press the seams open, using a point turner to get into the corners.

12. With wrong sides together, tuck the canvas support inside the wool bag to check the fit. If it's too large around the upper edge to lie smoothly, take slightly deeper side seams, tapering back to the original stitching before you reach the lower corners. Tuck the canvas inside the bag and fit into the bag corners. Turn the strap carriers down and topstitch 1¾ inches from the upper edge of the bag, catching the canvas in the stitching (Figure 8). Backstitch at the beginning and end of the stitching.

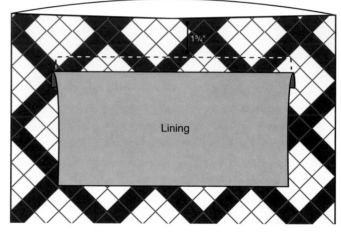

1¾"

Lining

Figure 8
Turn carrier out of way and stitch bag to canvas.

13. Align the raw edge of each strap carrier with the raw edge of the bag and machine-baste the layers together ¼ inch from the raw edges. A "bubble" will form in the strap carrier.

14. Tuck the bag into the lining with right sides together—it will be a snug fit because the lining is shorter than the bag. Pin the upper raw edges of the lining and bag together and stitch ½ inch from the raw edges.

15. Carefully turn the bag right side out through the opening in the lining bottom seam. Turn in the opening edges and press. Machine-stitch the folded edges together. Turn the bag wrong side out and hand-tack the lining to the canvas at each bottom corner to anchor the lining. Turn the bag right side out. Tuck the lining into the bag and press the upper edges between the strap carriers.

16. Working from the inside, edgestitch the lining to the bag from carrier edge to carrier edge (Figure 9). Use thread in the bobbin to match or blend into the bag fabric. Pin the strap carrier layers together close to the upper folded edge and topstitch ¾ inches from the fold.

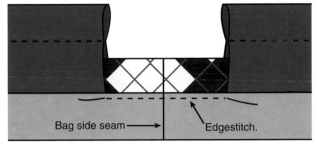

Figure 9
Topstitch ¾" from upper edges of carriers.

17. For the straps, cut two 32-inch-long pieces of ⅜-inch-wide elastic. Position a piece of elastic on the wrong side of each strap with one edge along the raw edge of a 30-inch-long strip and stitch through the center of the elastic. Turn the elastic onto the wrong side of the strip and press, using a press cloth to protect the

fabric. Turn the remaining raw edge of the suede strip in to meet the elastic and press. Fold the turned edge onto the suede-covered elastic and stitch in place through the center of the strip (Figure 10).

Figure 10
Cover elastic with suede for straps.

18. Thread a strap through each strap carrier using a bodkin or safety pin. On each strap, bring the strap ends together with right sides together (turned edge is the underside of the strap). Stitch through all layers close to the suede raw edges. **Note:** *Before stitching, make sure you haven't twisted the strap inside the carrier.* Backstitch and stitch forward again several times and trim the excess elastic ¼ inch from the strap ends. Pull the straps through the carrier to hide the elastic ends inside.

19. Gather the carriers on the straps to the desired fullness and stitch several times through the carrier edges and straps at each end of each carrier to secure. ●

FIELD OF FLOWERS

DESIGN BY MARTA ALTO

Classic linen is the perfect backdrop for your favorite machine-embroidered flowers on this simply shaped bag.

INSTRUCTIONS

Project Note: *All seam allowances are ¼ inch wide.*

Cutting

• From the nonwoven synthetic suede, cut one 1½ x 45-inch strip for the strap and front closure. Cut two

FINISHED SIZE

9¾ x 14¼ inches, including the welting

MATERIALS

• ½ yard 45-inch-wide linen or rayon/linen suiting
• ⅙ yard nonwoven synthetic suede in contrasting or matching color
• ½ yard light-colored firmly woven cotton for lining
• 1 yard 22-inch-wide medium-weight fusible weft-insertion interfacing
• ½ yard 22-inch-wide light-weight fusible weft-insertion or knit interfacing
• ½ yard paper-backed fusible web
• ⅓ yard polyester fleece
• 3½ yards ¼- or ⁵⁄₁₆-inch-diameter cotton filler cord for piping
• All-purpose thread to match fabrics

• Pattern tracing paper or cloth
• Tailor's chalk or air-soluble marking pen
• Floral embroidery design of your choice (OESD #44 from the Watercolor Floral Collection used for project)
• Rayon or polyester machine-embroidery thread
• Bobbin thread
• Temporary spray adhesive
• Medium-weight tear-away stabilizer
• 2-inch-diameter buckle for closure
• 2 purse rings for strap attachment
• Rotary cutter, mat and ruler
• Computerized sewing machine with embroidery unit and hoop
• Zipper foot
• Basic sewing tools and equipment

1½ x 33-inch strips for the strap and welting. Set the scraps aside for now.
• Apply medium-weight interfacing to the wrong side of the linen following the manufacturer's directions.
• Enlarge the bag, bag facing and lining pattern pieces (Figure 1) on pattern tracing paper and cut out.

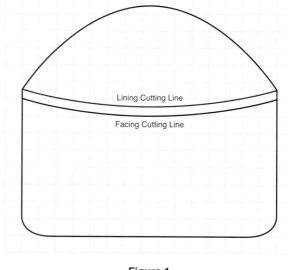

Lining Cutting Line

Facing Cutting Line

Figure 1
Bag Pattern
1 square = 1"

• Position the bag pattern on the right side of the linen. Pin in place and trace around the pattern with tailor's chalk or air-soluble marking pen to mark the cutting lines for the bag front. Repeat for the bag back. Remove the pattern piece but do not cut out the bag pieces. Instead, cut an oversize rectangle beyond the bag outlines so that you can hoop the piece for embroidering on the

machine. Mark the positions for the embroidery on the bag front and back.

- From the remaining linen, cut two bag facings.
- Cut two bag lining pieces each from the lining fabric, the lightweight fusible interfacing, the polyester fleece and the fusible web. Trim ¼ inch from the upper edge of the fleece.
- Cut two bag facings from the lightweight interfacing.

Assembly

1. Hoop the bag front with the tear-away stabilizer and embroider as desired. If you have a second sewing machine, prepare the piping and straps while the embroidery machine stitches out the design.

2. To make the piping for the bag outer edge, apply a light coat of temporary spray adhesive to the wrong side of one 1½ x 33-inch suede strip. Place a 34-inch-long piece of cotton filler cord in the center of the strip and wrap the suede around the cord with raw edges even. Use your fingers to smooth the suede in place. Attach the zipper foot and adjust to the right of the needle. Stitch as close to the cord as possible (Figure 2). If necessary, trim the seam allowance to ¼ inch.

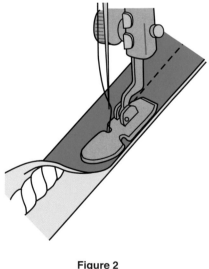

Figure 2
Stitch close to cord.

3. For the strap, lap one short end of the remaining 33-inch-long strip ¼ inch over a short end of the 45-inch-long strip; edgestitch the layers together. Apply temporary adhesive to the wrong side, center the remaining cotton filler cord on the strip and wrap as you did for the piping. Stitch as close to the cord as possible and *trim the excess suede close to the stitching*. Cut a

14-inch-long piece from the longer part of the strap for the decorative loop closure.

4. Fold the 14-inch piece in half and loop it through the buckle. Pull the ends through the loop to attach the piece to the buckle. Set aside.

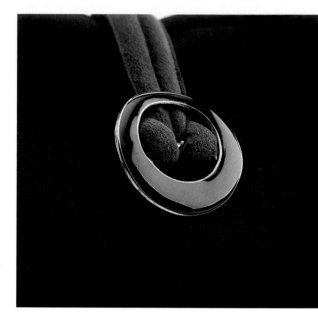

5. From the suede scraps, cut two ¾ x 12-inch strips. Apply spray adhesive to the wrong side of one strip and place the other one on top with wrong sides together. Stitch close to both long edges and again ⅛ inch from the first two rows of stitching. Stitch again through the center of the strip. Cut the strip into two equal lengths. Cut one piece in half lengthwise and set aside for the strap wraps. Cut the remaining piece in half crosswise for two ¾ x 3-inch strips. Loop each 3-inch-long strip through a ring and stitch the raw ends together (Figure 3).

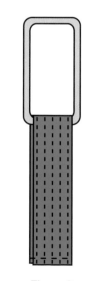

Figure 3
Wrap strip around metal ring; baste ends together.

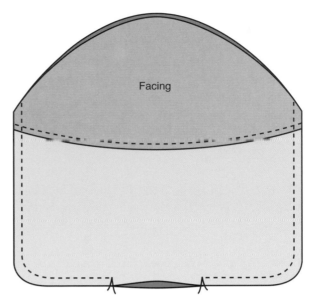

Figure 4
Sew facing/lining units together.

6. Pull the strap through one of the rings and whipstitch the raw ends together by hand. Position the join 1 inch above one of the rings; wrap one of the narrow strips of suede cut in step 5 around the join several times to hide it. Hand-sew in place. Repeat at the opposite side of the doubled strap Set aside.

7. Apply the fusible interfacing to the wrong side of the bag lining pieces.

8. Optional: From the remaining lining, cut and assemble pockets of the desired sizes and shapes, and sew in place on the lining pieces.

9. With right sides facing, sew a bag facing to the upper edge of each lining piece. Press the seams toward the lining.

10. With right sides facing, sew the lining/facing units together ⅜ inch from the side and bottom edges leaving an 8-inch opening in the bottom seam for turning (Figure 4). Do not turn the lining right side out. The lining will be slightly smaller than the bag so it will fit smoothly inside the finished bag.

11. When the embroidery is completed on the fabric for the bag front and bag, reposition the pattern piece over each embroidery. Take care to center the design between the seam lines. Pin in place and cut out the bag front. Repeat for the bag back.

12. Apply the fusible web to the wrong side of the polyester fleece pieces following the manufacturer's directions. Remove the backing paper and apply the batting to the wrong side of the bag front and back pieces. Fuse in place.

13. With right sides together and raw edges even, machine-baste the piping to the side and bottom edges of the bag front. Use contrasting thread in the bobbin and attach the zipper foot. Adjust it to the right of the needle and stitch close to the cord.

14. With right sides facing, sew the bag back to the back front. Stitch with the wrong side of the bag front on top so you can see the basting. Stitch just inside the basting a bit closer to the cord. Turn the bag right side out and finger-press the linen along the suede piping.

15. Position the short ends of the ring loops at the upper edge of the bag to either side of the piping with raw edges even; baste (Figure 5).

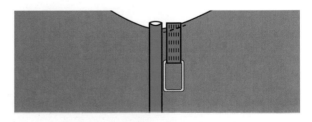

Figure 5
Baste loops to bag upper edge.

16. Place the bag inside the lining with right sides together and stitch ¼ inch from the upper edge. Turn the bag right side out through the opening in the lining. Turn in the opening edges of the lining and press. Edgestitch together. Tuck the lining into the bag and press the upper edge. Stitch close to the edge, breaking the stitching at the piping edges. Don't try to stitch over the piping.

17. Position the cord ends of the decorative closure on the bag back 4¼ inches below the upper finished edge. Pin in place.

18. From the remaining suede scrap, cut one 1½ x 2-inch piece and round off the corners of one short end to shape the decorative tab. Apply a light coat of spray adhesive to the wrong side of the tab and position over the cord ends (Figure 6). Stitch close to the edges over all layers; stitch slowly over the cord ends to avoid breaking the sewing machine needle. ●

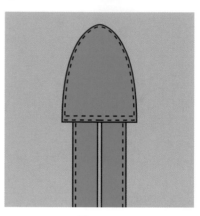

Figure 6
Sew tab in place, enclosing the closure cord ends on back of bag.

FLAP HAPPY

DESIGN BY BARBARA WEILAND

It's as flirty and feminine as it can be. Shaped suede flaps in assorted lengths are arranged in overlapping rows to create the layered "skirt" on this happy-go-lucky lined bag.

INSTRUCTIONS

Project Note: *Use ¼-inch-wide seams unless otherwise directed.*

Cutting

- Enlarge the pattern pieces (Figure 1) on pattern tracing paper.
- Cut one each front and back from suede and from canvas.
- From the suede, cut two strips each 3½ x 22 inches for

the straps. For the flaps, begin by cutting five of each flap size; you can cut more if needed. Also cut two each of the following pieces: mini flap, bag collar, facing, and large and small triangles (strap attachments). Cut one

FINISHED SIZE

13 x 12 x 3½ inches

MATERIALS

- 1¼ yards nonwoven synthetic suede (see Note below)
- ⅜ yard 44- or 54-inch-wide cotton canvas or crisp woven fabric for interlining
- ¼ yard coordinating or contrasting lining
- ¼ yard lightweight fusible interfacing
- All-purpose thread to match fabrics
- Pattern tracing paper
- 2 overall strap loops for handle connectors, or substitute other metal rings or connectors
- Temporary spray adhesive
- Permanent fabric adhesive
- Water-soluble basting tape or narrow strips of double-stick fusible web
- Optional: 1 or more magnetic snap sets
- Rotary cutter, mat and ruler
- Press cloth
- Basic sewing tools and equipment

Note: *Do not use woven suede-cloth, as the raw edges of flaps cut from woven fabric will ravel.*

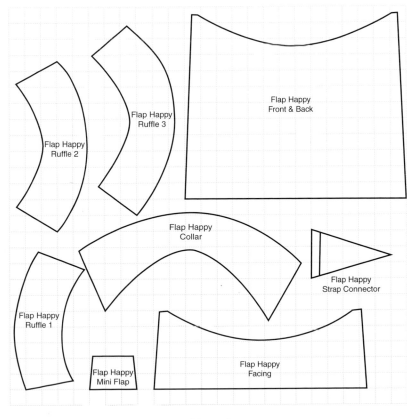

Figure 1
Patterns for Flap Happy.
1 square = 1"

1¼ x 30-inch suede strip for the upper-edge finish and one ¼ x 44-inch strip of suede for the strap wraps. Cut one 3 x 7-inch strip for the strap tubes.

• Cut two lining pieces.

• Cut two facings from the fusible interfacing. Apply to the wrong side of the suede facings, using a press cloth to protect the suede.

Assembly

1. Sew a lining piece to the lower edge of each bag facing. Press the seam toward the lining, protecting the suede with a press cloth. Topstitch ¼ inch from the seam line through all layers. With right sides together, sew the lining/facing units together along the side and bottom edges. Set the lining aside (Figure 2).

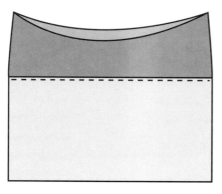

Figure 2
Prepare lining.

2. Fold each strap strip in half with right sides together and long edges even. Stitch ¼ inch from the raw edges and turn the resulting tubes right side out. DO NOT PRESS. With the seam centered on the underside of each strap, stack the straps one on top of the other and stitch together at the short ends ¼ inch from the raw edges. Set the straps aside.

Note: *Do not press the straps at any time so they remain "soft" tubes.*

3. Apply a light coat of temporary spray adhesive to the wrong side of the suede bag front and back pieces, and smooth into place on corresponding canvas pieces.

4. With right sides together, sew the bag front and back together at the side seams. Finger-press the seams open and topstitch with a narrow, medium-width zigzag stitch that crosses the seam line and bites into the seam allowances on both sides (Figure 3). Sew the front and back collar pieces together in the same manner.

Figure 3
Zigzag over seam lines.

5. Choose a shaped flap and straighten the upper curved edge so the lower edge "ruffles." Position it 1½ inches from the upper edge, wrapping it over a side seam to the opposite side of the bag. Pin in place. Add another flap to the opposite side, using a different-size flap and positioning it 1 inch from the upper edge, with varying amounts extending over the seam line to the front and back of the bag. Pin in place. Working over the sewing-machine free arm, straight-stitch the upper raw edge of each flap in place. Backstitch at the beginning and end of each one and pull the threads to the canvas side before clipping (Figure 4).

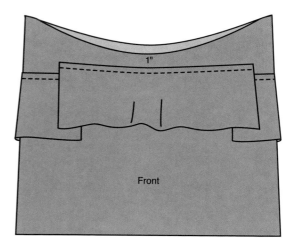

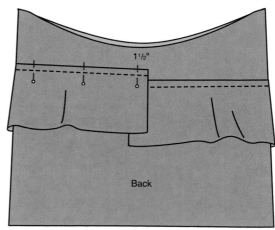

Figure 4
Sew flaps to bag front and back.

6. Arrange flaps row by row in an overlapping fashion to cover the bag front and back from top to bottom; pin in place temporarily near the upper raw edge of each one. You will need at least five rows of flaps, and the last layer should extend at least to the bottom edge or ¼ inch past it. It's a good idea to pin all remaining flaps in place and play with the positioning until you are happy with the final appearance. Leave the pinned assemblage in your sewing room and go back to evaluate it the next day before finalizing the flap placement. It is likely to look better to you after you have left it for a while. When you are satisfied with the arrangement, stitch each flap in place.

Note: *Every Flap Happy bag made from this pattern will probably be a bit different due to the flap placement.*

7. Position the collar on the top of the bag at the upper edge. The lower edge should overlap the uppermost flaps. Center a small flap at the upper edge on each side of the bag, and machine-baste the flap and collar to the bag ¼ inch from the raw edges (Figure 5).

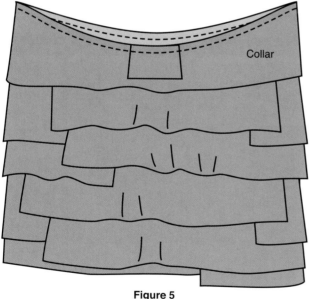

Figure 5
Sew collar and mini flap to upper edge of bag.

8. Turn the bag wrong side out and stitch the bottom edges together. Turn right side out and trim the lower edges of the bottom row of flaps if desired. On the bag shown, the flaps are about ¼ inch longer than the bag underneath so the bottom edge of the bag doesn't show.

9. Slip the facing/lining unit into the bag with raw edges and seam lines aligned. Machine-baste together ¼ inch from the raw edges.

10. Beginning and ending at one side seam, pin the 1¼-inch-wide suede strip to the right side of the bag with right sides together. Where the ends meet, overlap ¼ inch and trim away any excess strip. Stitch a scant ⅜ inch from the raw edges.

11. Turn the strip to the inside of the bag over the raw edges and use narrow water-soluble basting tape to secure the suede strip for stitching.

12. On the right side of the bag, stitch in the ditch of the binding seam, catching the underlayer in the stitching. On the inside, neatly trim the suede close to the stitching.

13. For the strap connectors, stack the triangles in pairs of one large and one small with right sides facing up. Stitch across each pair 1½ inches from the point (Figure 6).

14. Loop the point through the shaped end of an overall buckle with the stitching along the metal and stitch through all layers (see Figure 7). You may need to use a zipper foot or ¼-inch foot on the sewing machine.

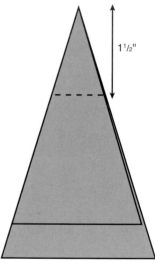

Figure 6
Stack and sew two triangles together.

15. Position a buckle with suede flap at each side seam and stitch in place at the lower edge of the binding (Figure 7).

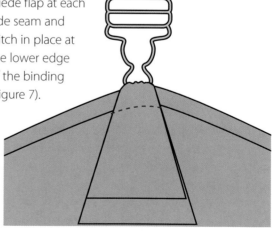

Figure 7
Stitch the connectors to the bag at side seams.

18. Pull the tubes down over the stitched ends to cover them. It will be a snug fit and will take a little work to pull the tubes tight.

19. Apply one or more magnetic snaps to the upper edge of the bag, hiding the prongs under the upper row of flaps on the outside of the bag. Three snaps are recommended for the most secure closure.

20. Use the ¼-inch-wide suede strip to tightly wrap the strap connector triangles several times just below the metal loop. Trim the excess, tuck the end under the wraps and use a drop of permanent fabric glue to secure the end. ●

16. Fold the 3 x 7-inch suede strip in half lengthwise with right sides together and long edges even. Stitch ¼ inch from the raw edges and turn the resulting tube right side out. From the tube, cut two 3¼-inch lengths. Center the seam on the underside of each tube and fold each one in half with raw edges even. Stitch ¼ inch from the ends to create a finished tube. Slide a tube onto each end of the doubled straps you prepared earlier and push them several inches up and away from the strap raw ends.

17. Loop the strap ends through the buckle bars and stitch the raw end to the underside of the layered straps (Figure 8).

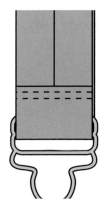

Figure 8
Slip strap ends through the bars
or the overall loops. Stitch.

PUR-SUEDE ME

DESIGN BY KELLY LAWRENCE

Faux suede and vinyl get a totally feminine treatment with flirty bows. Polka-dot ribbon cinches add a little sass to this roomy, lined bag, complete with an easy-to-stitch, zipped, inner pocket.

INSTRUCTIONS

Project Note: Use ½-inch-wide seam allowances unless otherwise directed.

Cutting

• From the synthetic suede, cut two 11 x 18-inch

FINISHED SIZE

12 x 7¾ x 5 inches

MATERIALS

• ½ yard nonwoven synthetic suede
• ½ yard lining fabric
• ⅛ yard 54-inch-wide vinyl
• 3¼ yards 1-inch-wide grosgrain ribbon
• ⅜ yard heavyweight fusible nonwoven interfacing
• 4 x 22-inch strip paper-backed fusible web
• 3 x 7-inch rectangle medium-weight fusible interfacing for lining pocket
• 5-inch-long zipper for inside pocket (see Note)
• All-purpose thread to match fabric and ribbon

• Air-soluble marking pen
• 1 magnetic snap closure
• Press cloth
• Point presser and tailor's clapper
• 6 x 14-inch piece foam-core board for bottom support
• Permanent fabric adhesive
• Paper clips
• Basting tape
• Rotary cutter, mat and ruler
• Craft knife with fresh blade
• Basic sewing tools and equipment

Note: If a 5-inch-long zipper is not available, shorten a 7-inch-long zipper by bartacking over the zipper coil 2 inches above the metal bottom stop. Cut the excess zipper ½ inch below the bar tack.

rectangles and two 1 x 21-inch strips for the straps.

• From the lining fabric, cut two 10¾ x 17½-inch rectangles and one 5 x 6-inch rectangle for the pocket lining.

• From the ribbon, cut two 34-inch-long pieces for the ribbon cinches and two 21-inch-long pieces for the straps.

• From the vinyl, cut one 1 x 34-inch strip for the inside facing and four 3-inch squares. Cut four 2-inch vinyl squares for the outside of the bag. On the wrong side of each 2-inch vinyl square, draw a 1-inch square in the center. Use the craft knife to carefully cut out center along the lines.

• From the fusible web, cut two ¾ x 21-inch-long strips for the handles.

• From the heavyweight fusible nonwoven interfacing, cut two 10¾ x 17¾-inch rectangles and two 1½-inch squares.

• From the foam-core board, cut a 4⅞ x 12½-inch-rectangle for the bottom support.

Assembly

1. Center a piece of heavyweight fusible interfacing, fusible side down, on the wrong side of each 11 x 18-inch synthetic suede rectangle. Fuse in place following the manufacturer's directions. Use a press cloth to protect the suede surface from iron imprints whenever fusing or pressing is required.

2. At the lower edge of each bag rectangle corner, mark and cut out a 3-inch square. With right sides facing, sew the bag

front and back together along the side and bottom edges (Figure 1). Press the seams open over the point presser. Use the tailor's clapper to set the press while the suede cools.

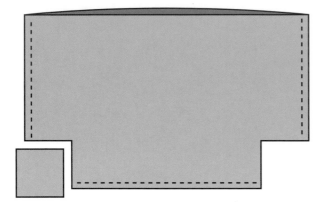

Figure 1
Cut a 3" square from each lower corner of bag and lining rectangles. Stitch side and bottom seams.

3. Mark and trim a 3-inch square from the lower corner of each lining rectangle. Set aside.

4. Fold each bottom corner of the bag with the side and bottom seam lines aligned. Stitch ½ inch and ⅜ inch from the raw edges (Figure 2). Turn the bag right side out.

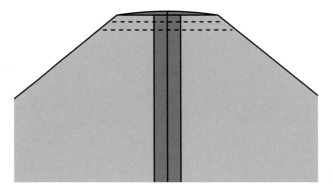

Figure 2
Align seam lines and stitch bottom corners.

5. Apply a generous coat of fabric adhesive to one side of the foam-core board and insert, glue side down, into the bottom of the bag. Press firmly in place and allow to dry while you prepare the lining.

6. Center the 3 x 7-inch fusible interfacing rectangle on the wrong side of one lining piece as shown in Figure 3. Fuse in place. Draw a ⅝ x 5-inch rectangle in the center of the interfacing. Stitch on the lines. Slash through the center of the stitched box and clip to the corners.

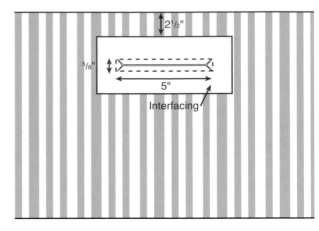

Figure 3
Stitch on lines; slash through center and to corners.

7. Refer to Figure 4 for steps 7–9. Turn under and press the cut edges along the stitching. Center the zipper under the opening and edgestitch in place.

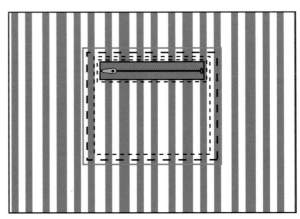

Figure 4
Stitch pocket in place (pocket is on wrong side of lining).

8. Pink or serge-finish all four edges of the 5 x 6-inch lining pocket rectangle. Position it face down over the zipper on the wrong side of the lining with the upper edges ¾ inch above the opening edge. Baste in place ¼ inch from the finished edges.

9. On the right side of the lining, stitch on top of the previous stitching along the upper edge and the short ends of the zipper opening, continuing down and around the pocket as shown in Figure 4.

10. On the wrong side of each lining rectangle, center and fuse a 1½-inch square of interfacing for the snap closure reinforcement. Following the manufacturer's directions, install the magnetic snap at the center on the right side of each lining piece (Figure 5) with the center of the snap 1½ inches from the upper edge of the lining.

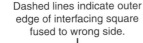
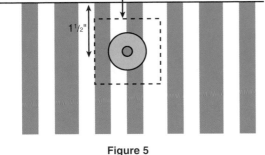

Dashed lines indicate outer
edge of interfacing square
fused to wrong side.

1½"

Figure 5
Apply snap closure to upper edges of lining panels.

11. Sew the lining pieces together and finish the bottom corners as you did for the bag (Figure 2, step 4). Do not turn the lining right side out.

12. Apply a line of fabric adhesive in the center along the length of the foam-core board inside the bag. Insert the lining and smooth into place with the bottom seam allowance in the glue. Allow to dry.

13. Pin the upper edges of the bag and lining together and machine-baste ¼ inch from the raw edges.

14. Apply a strip of fusible interfacing to the wrong side of each 21-inch-long piece of ribbon. Remove the backing paper and fuse each ribbon to the wrong side of a 21-inch-long suede strip. Stitch close to both long edges of each strap.

15. With an air-soluble marker, measure and mark a placement line ¾ inch from each end of each strap. With the suede side of the straps against the lining and the ¾-inch marks at the bag upper edge, position the straps 5 inches from each side seam. Use basting tape to secure them for stitching.

16. Apply a strip of basting tape to the wrong side of the vinyl facing through the center of the strip; remove the protective paper. Beginning at one side seam on the inside of the bag, position one raw edge of the strip even with the upper raw edges. Use paper clips at the upper edges to hold the layers together if necessary. Run your fingers along the center of the strip to adhere the basting tape to the lining. Stitch close to both long edges of the vinyl strip, removing paper clips as you reach them. Be sure to use thread in the bobbin to match the suede.

17. On the outside of the bag, center a 2-inch vinyl square beneath each strap with the upper edge of the square ½ inch from the bag upper edge. Use basting tape between the layers to secure the square for stitching.

18. Center a 3-inch square of vinyl under each 2-inch square on the inside of the bag and secure with basting tape. With thread to match the vinyl in the needle and bobbin, stitch close to the outer and inner cut edges of the vinyl squares on the bag right side. Working on the rotary cutting mat, use the craft knife to cut out the center square in each of the larger squares (Figure 6).

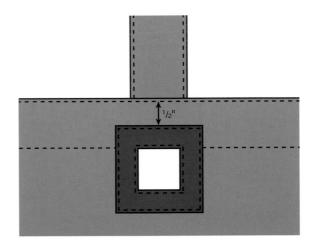

½"

Figure 6
Stitch vinyl squares in place; cut out center of backing square even with inner cut edges.

19. Tuck the side seams into the bag so they just meet the square openings. Lace a ribbon through each set of squares and tie in a bow. Hand-tack the knot layers together to secure each bow if desired. Cut the ribbon ends at an angle. ●

SCARF TRICK

DESIGN BY KAREN DILLON

Turn a classic fringed wool plaid scarf into a suede-trimmed dressmaker bag. A suede panel also protects the bottom of the finished bag.

INSTRUCTIONS

Project Notes: *Use ½-inch-wide seam allowances, unless otherwise indicated. Apply fusible interfacings as directed, following the manufacturer's directions. Use a press cloth to protect the suede and the wool from heat damage.*

FINISHED SIZE

13 x 12 x 3½ inches

MATERIALS

- One wool plaid scarf with fringe at both ends
- 1 yard 45-inch-wide fabric for lining
- ¼ yard synthetic suede (or a 7 x 36-inch scrap)
- ⅞ yard heavyweight fusible interfacing for bag body, bottom panel and shoulder strap
- ½ yard medium-weight fusible interfacing for flap, shoulder strap and trim
- 1 metal buckle with 1½-inch-wide opening
- 1-inch square of hook-and-loop tape for closure
- ¼-inch-wide fusible web
- All-purpose thread to match fabrics
- Press cloth
- Topstitching or denim needle, size 90 or 100
- Basic sewing tools and equipment

Cutting

- From each end of the scarf, cut a 12-inch-long piece (length includes the fringe) for the flap and flap facing. From the remaining scarf, cut a 14 x 29-inch piece for the bag body and two 4½ x 13¼-inch rectangles for the side panels. Take care to cut these so they match the plaid in the body of the bag if possible.
- From the synthetic suede, cut one 3½ x 14-inch rectangle for the bag bottom panel, one 1¾ x 14-inch strip for the buckle strap (you may need to adjust the width for the buckle you are using), two 2 x 13-inch strips for the upper band and one 2¼ x 32-inch strip for the shoulder strap.
- From the heavyweight fusible interfacing, cut one 13¾ x 28¾-inch rectangle for the bag body, two 4¼ x 13-inch strips for the side panels, and one 3⅜ x 13¾-inch strip for the suede bottom panel.
- From the medium-weight fusible interfacing, cut two 8½ x 13¾-inch pieces for the flap and flap facing, one 1¾ x 14-inch strip for the buckle strap, two 1¾ x 12¾-inch strips for the upper band and two 2 x 31¾-inch strips for the straps.
- From the lining fabric, cut two 14 x 15-inch pieces and two 4½ x 13¼-inch pieces for the side panels.
- Apply fusible interfacings to the wrong side of each corresponding bag and suede piece. Interfacing strips were cut slightly smaller than suede pieces. Center them on the pieces before fusing. This prevents edges from showing at the suede raw edges. Note that the interfacing must end slightly above the fringe on the flap and flap facing pieces so it doesn't show when the flap is turned right side out after the side seams are stitched.

Assembly

1. Fold the 2¼ x 32-inch suede strip in half lengthwise with wrong sides (interfaced) together and press firmly. Use a press cloth to protect the suede. Edgestitch along both long edges of the strap. Set aside.

2. With right sides facing and raw edges even, sew the flap to the flap facing at the side edges. Turn right side out and press. Tuck a strip of ¼-inch-wide fusible web between the flap layers just above the fringe and fuse. Topstitch the layers together just above the fringe, if desired.

3. With the right side facing out, slip the interfaced 1¾ x 14-inch suede strip through the buckle and bring the short raw ends together. Machine-baste ¼ inch from the raw edge. Slip ¼-inch-wide strips of fusible web between

the layers at each long raw edge and fuse. Use a press cloth to protect the suede.

4. Center the buckle/band on one flap panel and edgestitch in place, ending the stitching on each long edge as close to the buckle as you can comfortably reach with the needle and presser foot (Figure 1).

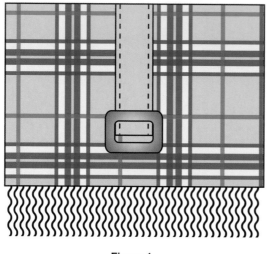

Figure 1
Stitch strap edge to flap.

5. With right sides together, stitch the 14-inch-long edges of the two 14 x 15-inch lining panels together; leave a 10-inch-long opening in the seam. Press the seam to one side. The resulting panel should measure 14 x 29 inches.

6. On the bag body, reinforce each long edge as shown in Figure 2. Use a shorter-than-average stitch length and stitch a scant ½ inch from the raw edges. Clip to the stitching. Repeat with the lining panel.

7. Position the suede bottom panel on the right side of the bag body between the clips and use narrow strips of fusible web to fuse the long edges in place. Edgestitch.

8. With right sides together, pin a bag side panel to each edge of the bag panel. The clips in the bag edges will allow you to turn the "corners" at the suede bottom panel. Stitch, pivoting at the corners. Press the seams open (Figure 3). Repeat with the lining. Do not turn the lining right side out.

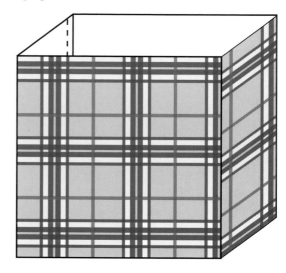

Figure 3
Sew bag to side panels.

9. Sandwich the strap ends between the two 2 x 13-inch suede strips ¾ inch in from the short ends and machine-stitch ⅜ inch from the long raw edges of the strip through all layers. Use strips of fusible web to hold the suede layers together. Fuse. Stitch close to the side and remaining raw edges (Figure 4).

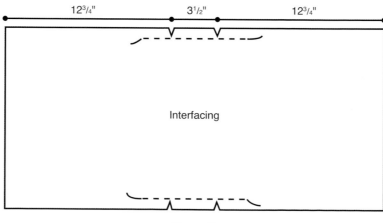

Figure 2
Reinforce edges and clip.

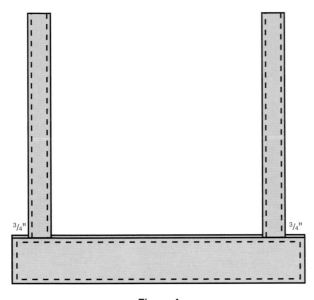

Figure 4
Sandwich strap ends between 2 suede strips.
Stitch layers together ³⁄₈" from lower edge.

10. With raw edges even, pin the suede band with the straps to the upper edge of the bag back. Stitch a scant ½ inch from the raw edges (Figure 5).

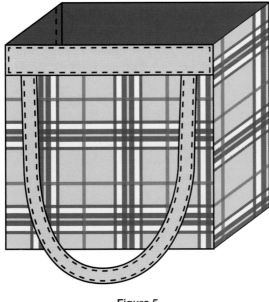

Figure 5
Baste suede strip to upper edge of bag panel.

11. With the buckle strap against the right side of the bag back, pin the flap to the upper edge of the bag. Machine-baste ³⁄₈ inch from the raw edges.

12. Tuck the bag with flap and straps inside the lining with seam lines and raw edges aligned; pin. Change the needle to the denim or topstitching needle. Stitch ¾ inch from the upper edge through all layers. Grade the seam at the back upper edge to eliminate bulk.

13. Carefully turn the bag right side out through the opening in the lining. Press the upper edge of the bag, rolling the lining to the inside so it doesn't show; edgestitch. Turn under and press the seam allowance at the opening edges in the lining. Machine-stitch the turned edges together.

14. Attach the hook half of the hook-and-loop tape to the underside of the flap under the buckle area. Flip the buckle out of the way when stitching. Smooth the flap into position on the bag front and mark the position for the loop tape. Stitch in place through all layers.

15. At the upper edge of each side panel, fold the panel in half with right sides together and pin. Stitch ½ inch from the fold, backstitching at the beginning and ending the stitching 1 inch from the upper edge. Backstitch.

16. Add a removable insert, cut to fit the bag bottom, to add support and maintain shape. ●

HOBO SOPHISTICATE

DESIGN BY CAROL ZENTGRAF

Inspired by an expensive designer handbag, this hobo-style bag is made of synthetic suede and lined with a fun-loving coordinating cotton print. Metal studs add fashion panache to the shaped outer pocket.

FINISHED SIZE

11 x 10 x 2 inches, excluding handles

MATERIALS

- ⅝ yard 45-inch-wide nonwoven synthetic suede fabric
- ½ yard 45-inch-wide cotton print fabric for lining
- ¾ yard 22-inch-wide heavy-weight fusible interfacing
- Pattern tracing paper or cloth
- Water-soluble marking pen
- 15 size 40 flat-head studs (plus extras for testing on scraps)
- Stud-setting tool
- 16-inch-long piece 1-inch-wide stiff waistband interfacing
- 12-inch-long zipper
- 2 (1¾-inch-diameter) metal rings
- Permanent fabric adhesive
- Self-adhesive, double-sided basting tape
- Rotary cutter, mat and ruler
- Basic sewing tools and equipment

INSTRUCTIONS

Project Notes: *Use ½-inch-wide seam allowances. Before beginning this project, read* **Smooth Sewing** *on page 89 for tips on sewing with synthetic suede.*

Cutting

- Enlarge the pattern pieces (Figure 1) on pattern tracing paper and cut out.
- Pin the pattern pieces to a single layer of suede, *placing the pins within the ½-inch-wide seam allowances only.* Cut two bags, two pockets, one gusset and one zipper panel. For the strap, use the rotary-cutting tools to cut one 2½ x 18-inch strip.
- From the cotton print for the lining, cut two bags and one gusset.
- From the interfacing, cut two bags, one pocket panel and one gusset.

Assembly

1. Apply the interfacing to the wrong side of the bag front, back and gusset. Use a press cloth to protect the suede and avoid leaving the iron in one place too long to prevent the steam vents from imprinting on the suede. Do not slide the iron. Apply interfacing to the wrong side of one pocket piece.

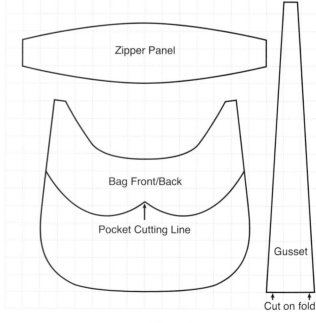

Figure 1
Bag Pattern
1 square = 1"

2. Refer to Figure 2 for steps 2 and 3. Mark the position for the first stud at the center point of the interfaced pocket, ⅝ inch below the point. Make dots to mark the positions for the positions for six studs on each side of the center mark, spacing the marks ⅞ inch apart and ½ inch from the upper edge (Figure 2). Follow the directions with the stud-setting machine to apply the studs at each mark. ***Note:*** *When the studs are applied there will be ½ inch of space between them.*

Figure 2
Add studs and then edgestitch pocket pieces together.
Baste outer edges together.

3. Apply basting tape along the cut edges of the interfaced pocket panel. Remove the paper backing and adhere to the remaining pocket panel with wrong sides together and edges even. Topstitch the upper edges together close to the edge. Machine-baste ¼ inch from the remaining edges.

4. Use basting tape to adhere the pocket to the lower edge of one bag panel with edges aligned. Machine-baste ¼ inch from the raw edges.

5. On the zipper panel, draw a ½ x 11-inch box in the center and carefully cut out the box. Apply basting tape to both long edges of the box on the wrong side of the suede. Remove the protective tape. With right sides up, center the zipper panel over the zipper with the zipper pull at one short end of the box. The zipper is longer than the opening. Stitching from the right side, stitch around the opening, close to the suede edge (Figure 3). Stitch slowly over the end of the zipper where the box crosses the zipper coil.

Figure 3
Center zipper under opening and edgestitch in place.

6. With right sides facing, sew the upper edge of the front/pocket panel to one long edge of the zipper panel. Use basting tape to hold the layers together for stitching. Trim the seam to ¼ inch, clip the curves and finger-press the seam allowance toward the front panel. Topstitch in place close to the seam line. Sew the remaining bag panel to the remaining edge of the zipper panel in the same manner.

7. Mark the center of each panel lower edge and the center of the gusset. Aligning the center marks, use basting tape to adhere the gusset to the front panel with the upper ends of the gusset ending 1½ inches above the upper edge of the bag (Figure 4).

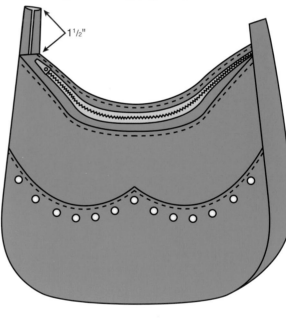

Figure 4
Sew gusset to bag front and back
with 1½" extending at upper edges.

8. Repeat with the remaining panel. Trim the seam allowances, clip the curves and turn right side out. Tuck the short raw ends of the zipper panel down into the bag against the wrong side of the gusset extensions.

9. On each gusset extension, turn the raw edges to the wrong side so they meet in the center; use fabric adhesive to glue them in place. Place a metal ring on each extension and wrap the extension end to the underside, creating a loop. Stitch the end to the zipper panel ½ inch from the end of the zipper opening; trim excess extension fabric.

10. On the wrong side of the lining zipper panel, draw the box as you did for the suede. Stitch ⅛ inch outside the marked box all around. Cut through the center and clip to the corners. Turn under and press along the stitching, and then machine-stitch ⅛ inch from the turned edges (Figure 5).

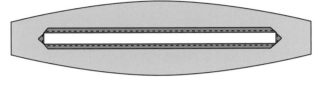

Figure 5
Edgestitch turned edges of opening.

11. Complete the lining assembly as for the bag assembly. Trim the gusset extensions so they extend ¼ inch above the finished lining. Do not turn the lining right side out.

12. Insert the lining in the handbag. Slipstitch or glue the zipper opening edges to the zipper tapes on the inside of the bag.

13. To make the strap, first draw a placement line on the wrong side along the center of the 2½ x 18-inch strip from one short end to the other. Position one long edge of the stiff waistband interfacing along the placement line. Use basting tape to adhere the other long edge to the suede. Wrap the remaining suede around the interfacing to encase it, and stitch ⅛ inch from both long edges of the strap.

14. Wrap the strap ends around the rings, adjusting the length as desired. Stitch in place and trim excess fabric if needed. Apply a stud through all layers of the strap above each ring. ●

Smooth Sewing

Follow these tips for sewing with synthetic suede to ensure a successful sewing experience.

• Avoid using pins or ripping seams where the holes will show. Instead, pin in the seam allowances only or use self-adhesive double-sided basting tape to hold layers together for stitching.

• Synthetic suede has a nap, and a right and wrong side. Use a "with-nap" layout when cutting pieces. However, you can angle the pieces on the fabric to keep yardage requirements to a minimum.

• Synthetic nonwoven suede doesn't ravel, so edges can be left cut instead of hemmed or seamed to reduce bulk.

• Use a Teflon presser foot on the machine for smoother stitching.

• Always use a press cloth when pressing and don't touch the iron directly to the fabric.

ROMANTIC
NOTIONS

Every woman needs a special bag for special occasions—one just large enough to carry the essentials and pretty enough to make a fashion statement.

BEADED AMULET

DESIGN BY STEPHANIE CORINA GODDARD

A purse tiny enough to wear as a necklace holds precious mementos or practical items such as tissue or lipstick. Embellishing a printed motif is a great way to get comfortable with hand beading.

INSTRUCTIONS

Project Note: *Use ⅜-inch-wide seam allowances.*

Cutting

- Apply fusible interfacing to the wrong side of the solid-color bag fabric.
- From the fused bag fabric, cut a 3¾ x 25-inch strip. From the strip, cut one 3¾ x 5¼-inch back, one 3¾ x 8¼-inch back lining and one 3¾ x 9½-inch front/front lining.
- From the novelty print for the flap, cut a 3¾-inch square, centering the desired motif in the square.
- From the batting, cut one 3¾ x 4¾-inch rectangle and one 3¾ x 8¼-inch rectangle.

ASSEMBLY

1. With right sides together, sew the flap to the upper edge of the 3¾ x 5¼-inch back rectangle. If desired, round off the flap corners as shown Figure 1 on page 92. Press the seam toward the flap. On the right side, position the ends of the cord at each side of the back just below the flap seam line. Wrap the cord into a small bundle and secure with a safety pin to the right side of the bag flap to keep it out of the way of the stitching in the next step.

FINISHED SIZE

4½ x 3 inches, excluding the cord

MATERIALS FOR ONE BAG

- ⅛ yard solid-color fabric for the bag (see Note at right)
- ⅛ yard very lightweight fusible weft-insertion interfacing
- 5 x 5-inch scrap of novelty print for the flap (see Note at right)
- Scrap of very thin (low-loft) batting
- 1 yard rattail cord
- Assorted seed beads and novelty beads
- Large safety pin
- All-purpose threads to match fabrics and beads
- Size 10 or 12 hand-sewing needle, approximately 1¼ inches long
- Basic sewing tools and equipment

Note: *Yardage is for 44/45-inch-wide fabric cut on the crosswise grainline; for directional prints or designs, you will need additional fabric. For the flap, choose a novelty print with a motif that is no larger than 2¾ inches square, or stamp a design on your flap with textile inks.*

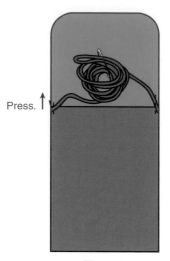

Figure 1
Baste cord to sides below flap seam.

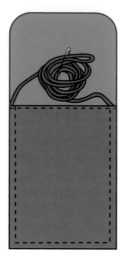

Figure 3
Baste lower panel to right side of flap/bag panel.

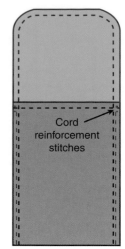

Figure 4
Stitch side seams.
Leave bottom open to turning.

2. With wrong sides together, fold the front/front lining in half to measure 3¾ x 4¾ inches. Press a firm crease at the fold. Unfold and position the 3¾ x 4¾-inch batting rectangle on the wrong side of the piece. Refold and edgestitch ⅛ inch from the fold to anchor the batting. Machine-baste ¼ inch from the raw edges at the short end of the layers (Figure 2).

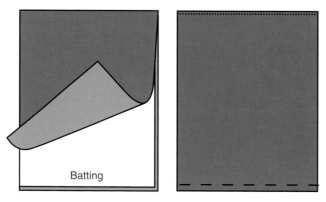

Figure 2
Add batting between layers. Baste edges together.

3. Place the prepared lining face down on the back of the bag back panel with the folded-and-stitched edge at the flap seam line. Machine-baste ¼ inch from all three raw edges (Figure 3).

4. Layer the remaining pieces with the batting on the bottom, the lining on top face up, and the right side of the flap facing the lining. Stitch ⅜ inch from the side and upper raw edges, leaving the bottom open for turning. Stitch again over the side seam at the cord locations several times for added security (Figure 4).

5. Turn the bag so the flap and front lining are both face up (hold onto the outermost layer of batting and the fabric layer closest to it, then turn all remaining layers through the opening). Smooth out the flap corners and press, avoiding placing the iron on the safety pin and cord. Stitch through all layers ⅜ and ¼ inch from the raw edges. Clip the corners and serge- or zigzag-finish the raw edges together (Figure 5).

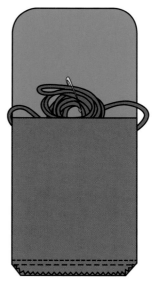

Figure 5
Stitch twice, trim, and zigzag or serge raw edge.

6. Release the safety pin. Turn the bag right side out and turn down the flap. Press firmly. Tuck the cord inside the bag until ready to wear the bag.

7. Embellish the flap with beading (see Sparkling Embellishments on page 94). ●

Sparkling Embellishments

Add a little sparkle to your finished bag with beads and a few easy stitches. Here's how:

1. Thread a fine, long hand-sewing needle with a single strand of regular sewing thread and tie a single overhand knot in the end.

2. From the lining side of the flap, poke the needle into the fabric, bringing it out at the desired position on the printed image. Tug gently on the thread to make it pop through the lining fabric and hide in the layers.

3. Take a tiny single stitch through the print fabric to secure the thread attachment and prevent the knot from working through the right side of the fabric.

4. Outline the print motif with seed beads. Pick up five seed beads and slide them down to the fabric surface. Lay the row of beads in position and poke the needle into the cloth at the end of the fifth bead. Skimming only through the print fabric layer, bring the needle out between the third and fourth beads. Run the needle through the fourth and fifth beads and then pick up five more seed beads (Figure 1).

Figure 1
Double back through fourth and fifth beads.

5. Repeat step 4 until the motif is completely outlined. End with a safety stitch. Tie an overhand knot close to the fabric surface and insert the needle into the cloth, exiting about 1 inch away. Gently tug on the thread until the knot pops between the layers and disappears. Trim the thread close to the fabric surface.

6. Highlight details with small rows of beads or with single beads. Sew individual beads with a backstitch (Figure 2).

Figure 2
Sew individual accent beads in place with backstitches.

7. To add a row of fringe to the flap edge, bring the needle out at the desired position at the flap edge and use the tip of the needle to pick up a column of beads, ending with a seed bead. Skipping the seed bead, run the needle back through the column and snug the beads to the fabric edge. Make a second safety stitch at the top of the column. Skim the needle between the fabric layers, emerging at the next location (Figure 3). Make a safety stitch before picking up beads for the next column.

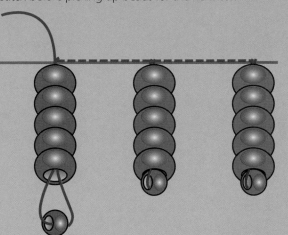

Figure 3
Add sead bead and then double
back through remaining beads for fringe.

Don't Lose Them

Pour a selection of beads onto a scrap of corduroy fabric. The ridges prevent the beads from rolling off the table and make sorting a breeze.

LACY BRIDAL WRISTLET

DESIGN BY BARBARA WEILAND

Scraps of lace and other bridal fabrics are perfect for this lovely bridal bag. A beaded tassel disguises the zipper pull on the lined bag that will hold the bride's essentials for the reception. Bridal attendants will love this bag, too, when made from fabrics that match or complement their gowns.

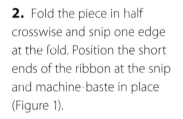

INSTRUCTIONS

Assembly

1. Apply the firm interfacing to the wrong side of the silk dupioni following manufacturer's directions.

Note: *It may be necessary to add a second piece of interfacing on top of the first for the desired firmness so the bag holds its finished shape.*

2. Fold the piece in half crosswise and snip one edge at the fold. Position the short ends of the ribbon at the snip and machine-baste in place (Figure 1).

FINISHED SIZE
7 x 7 x 7 inches

MATERIALS
- 7¾ x 15½-inch piece white silk dupioni or other bridal fabric
- 7¾ x 15½-inch piece white beaded lace
- 7¾ x 15½-inch piece very firm nonwoven fusible interfacing
- 7¾ x 15½-inch piece lining
- 14-inch-long piece white 1-inch-wide ribbon
- 7-inch white zipper
- 1 beaded tassel (about 2 inches long)
- White all-purpose thread
- Rotary cutter, mat and ruler
- Basic sewing tools and equipment

Center ribbon over snip here.

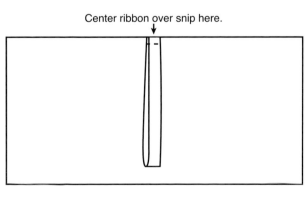

Figure 1
Fold ribbon in half and baste in place.

3. *Unzip the zipper* and position face down on the right side of the silk with the bottom stop ½ inch from the short end of the rectangle. Using a zipper foot, stitch the zipper tape to the rectangle as shown in Figure 2.

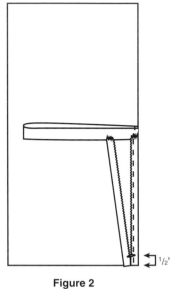

Figure 2
Stitch zipper to one half of long edge.

4. Fold the piece in half crosswise with right sides together so you can position the other half of the zipper on the lace-covered silk with the bottom stop ½ inch from the remaining short end and the upper ends of the two zipper tapes aligned. Stitch in place.

5. Press the fabric away from the zipper teeth, taking care to protect any beads or sequins on the lace from the heat of the iron (Figure 3).

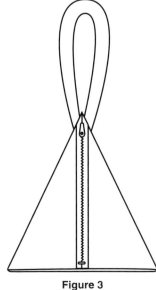

Figure 3
Completed Zipper

6. Turn under and press ⅜ inch along one long edge of the lining. Position along the stitching on the wrong side of the zipper tape and slipstitch in place. Make sure the folded edge of the lining is away from the zipper teeth so that it won't get caught in the zipper sliding action. Machine-baste the lining raw edges to the rectangle (trim away any excess lining to match the raw edges of the rectangle as needed). Zigzag-finish the long raw edge.

7. With the rectangle folded in half crosswise with right sides facing, stitch the edges opposite the zipper together (Figure 4). Press the seam open over a point presser and finish the seam edges with serging or zigzagging.

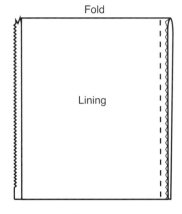

Figure 4
Stitch edges together.

8. Unzip the zipper. With right sides together, align the seam line on one side with the zipper seam line on the other side of the bag; pin. Stitch ⅜ inch from the raw edges. Stitch again ⅛ inch from the first stitching. Trim the seam close to the second stitching (Figure 5).

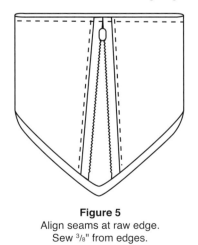

Figure 5
Align seams at raw edge.
Sew ³⁄₈" from edges.

9. Turn the bag right side out and decorate the zipper pull with ribbon, tassels, or strands of pearls or beads as desired. ●

LOVELY IN LACE

DESIGN BY JANIS BULLIS

Versatile enough for a dressy evening out or a day at the beach, this lovely lace backpack takes the ordinary to the sublime. Choose a beautiful lace—ours is real Cluny cotton lace—and line it with a pastel to show through for a hint of color. Just two simple pattern shapes are all it takes to make this pretty bag.

INSTRUCTIONS

Project Note: Use ½-inch-wide seam allowances. Press all seams open after stitching.

Cutting

• On pattern tracing paper, draw a 12 x 17-inch rectangle and round off the lower corners at one short end. Use a large dinner plate as the guideline for the corners (Figure 1).

FINISHED SIZE

11 x 16 x 2 inches

MATERIALS

All yardages are for 44/45-inch-wide fabric.

• 1 yard lace fabric with at least one scalloped edge (see Note at right)
• 1 yard medium-weight woven fabric for lining
• 2 yards ⅜-inch-diameter decorator cord for straps
• 1½ yards ¼-inch-diameter cord for drawstring
• ½ yard matching rattail cord

• All-purpose thread to match fabrics
• Pattern tracing paper or cloth
• Air-soluble marking pen or dressmaker's chalk
• Bodkin
• Masking tape
• Optional: permanent fabric glue
• Sleeve board or small rotary-cutting mat
• Basic sewing tools and equipment

Note: *If the lace you love does not have a scalloped edge, you can add one with trim. See Add a Scallop on page 100.*

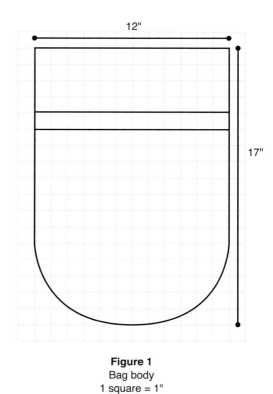

Figure 1
Bag body
1 square = 1"

• Use the pattern to cut four pieces from the lining. For the lining side panel, cut four 3 x 21½-inch strips.
• To cut the lace pieces, position the pattern piece so the scallop is along the short straight edge. Cut two bag bodies. From the remaining lace, cut two 3 x 21½-inch strips.

Assembly

1. With right sides facing, stitch two pieces of lining together along the upper edge. Press the seam open. Repeat with the remaining lining pieces.

2. Position a lace panel face up on top of each lining unit with raw edges even. Machine-baste a scant ½ inch from the raw edges (Figure 2).

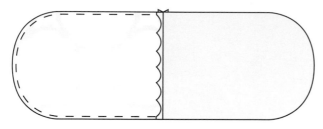

Figure 2
Baste lace panel to one lining panel of each pair.

3. Position the lace side panels on one set of lining panels and machine-baste a scant ½ inch from all raw edges.

4. With right sides facing, sew the short ends of the lace-covered lining panels together. Repeat with the remaining lining strips. Sew the resulting strips together at the short ends to make a large circle of fabric (Figure 3).

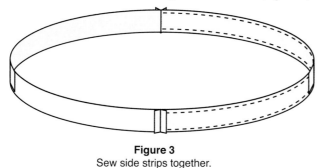

Figure 3
Sew side strips together.

5. With right sides together and seam lines matching as shown in Figure 4, pin the fabric circle to one of the lace/

Add a Scallop

If your lace doesn't have a scalloped edge, purchase ¾ yard of a flat lace trim with one scalloped edge. Sew it to one edge of the lace yardage by lapping it over the edge and stitching in place. Then cut the bag pieces as directed for lace with a built-in scalloped edge.

lining panels. Clip the strip as needed to ease it around the curved areas. Stitch.

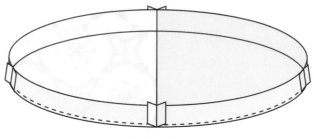

Figure 4
Sew side panel to bag/lining panel.

6. Sew the remaining bag piece to the remaining raw edge of the strip in the same manner, but leave a 6-inch-long opening in the lining and break the stitching as shown in Figure 5 to leave openings for the straps and drawstrings. Backstitch each time you start and stop the stitching.

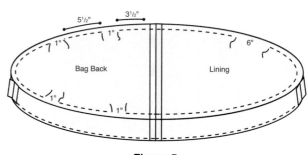

Figure 5
Leave openings in lining and bag back.

7. Carefully turn the bag right side out through the opening in the lining.

8. Smooth the lining inside the lace bag. Press the upper edges of the lining and edgestitch together if desired.

9. Working over a sleeve board or with a small rotary mat tucked inside the upper end, draw stitching lines 4 and 5 inches from the upper edge of the bag with an air-soluble marking pen or chalk that you can dust away. Pin the layers together, placing pins perpendicular to the stitching line. Stitch to create a casing tunnel for the drawstring (Figure 6 on next page).

10. At the halfway mark on the narrow cord, wrap the cord with masking tape. Then cut into two equal lengths. If the other cut ends are not protected in this manner, do so now. Draw one cord through the casing opening at one side seam using a bodkin. Feed it through the casing and then back out of the same opening. Repeat with remaining cord at the remaining side seam opening. Tie the cord ends on each side together in an overhand knot and wrap with rattail cord. Use stitches or permanent fabric glue to hold the cord in place. Remove the masking tape and allow the cut ends to fray and fluff out. **Optional:** *You can also embellish the cord ends with tassels or beads if you wish.*

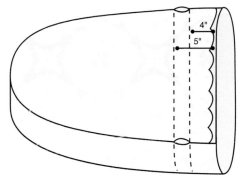

Figure 6
Stitch to make drawstring casing.

11. Tack the center of the remaining cord above the casing on the side of the bag with the lower openings in the side seam. Feed the cord ends into the openings in the side seams and pin in place. Try the bag on and adjust the cord lengths for a comfortable fit. Working through the 6-inch opening in the bag lining seam, complete the seams to catch the cord ends in the seams. Stitch across the cords several times to secure and stabilize them to take the weight of what you will carry in the backpack (Figure 7). Trim excess cord.

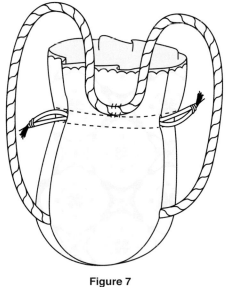

Figure 7
Tack cord above casing at center back.

12. Align the turned edges at the opening and edgestitch together to complete the lining. Tuck the lining back into the completed bag. ●

Laced in History

Cluny lace has been a favorite for centuries because of its light and airy quality, and beautiful intricate designs. It is made exclusively from twisted and braided threads with no fabric or net background. Flax and even human hair were the original fibers used to create it when it originated in pre-Christian times.

Sometimes referred to as pillow lace or bobbin lace, it was once constructed on a large stuffed pillow, placed on the maker's lap. First, straight pins were inserted in the pillow creating an intricate design. Then lengths of threads were tied to the pins and wound on wooden (originally bone) bobbins that served as weights hanging off the edges of the pillow as the maker twisted and braided the threads around the pins. The pins were repositioned and the twisting continued as the lace was slowly constructed.

Cluny lace fell out of favor for several centuries until a religious order of crafts people revived the ancient craft in the 19th century after visiting the Hotel de Cluny (now a lace museum). Today, most Cluny lace is machine-made from a durable cotton or linen fiber to create a sturdy, hard-wearing lace, seen in everything from household linens to the most elegant of clothing and accessory items.

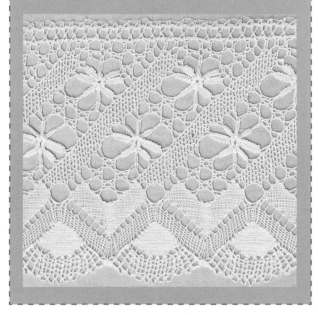

SCARF BE RUFFLED

DESIGN BY LUCY B. GRAY

Use a pretty scarf to make this flirty little shoulder bag. Choose one from your collection, buy a new one, or check out thrift stores for one that will work into your wardrobe.

INSTRUCTIONS

Cutting

- Trim away the hemmed edge on the scarf as close to the stitching as possible.
- Apply fabric protector to the scarf following the directions on the can.
- From the lining fabric, cut two 9½ x 11-inch rectangles.

- Using rotary-cutting tools, cut the scarf into six 3⅞-inch-wide strips. Set four strips aside and cut four 8-inch-long strips from the remaining two strips.
- From the coordinating solid fabric, cut one 2¾ x 20-inch strip for row 1. Cut two 3 x 20-inch strips for rows 2 and 3. Cut one 3½ x 20-inch strip for row 4. Label the strips to identify the rows.

FINISHED SIZE

10 x 10 x 1½ inches, excluding strap

MATERIALS

- 24-inch square silk or rayon scarf
- ¼ yard medim-weight fabric in coordinating color for bag body
- ½ yard lining fabric
- 11 x 24-inch rectangle polyester fleece
- All-purpose sewing thread to match scarf
- Lightweight tear-away stabilizer
- Temporary spray adhesive
- Spray-on fabric protector
- 1 magnetic snap set
- 32-inch metal chain suitable for bag handle
- 2½-inch-diameter metal O rings
- Large decorative button with shank
- ½-inch-diameter button
- Recycled earring
- 4-inch jewelry chain
- 4-inch-long decorative tassel
- Optional: 32 small teardrop beads
- 2 to 3 small jump rings
- 1 x 3-inch piece of milk-jug plastic for closure reinforcement
- 4 x 8-inch piece of cardboard
- Quick-drying craft glue
- Fine-tip permanent marking pen
- Pencil
- Ruler
- Rotary cutter, mat and ruler
- Basic sewing tools and equipment

Assembly

1. Finish the short ends of the scarf strips with a tiny zigzag stitch. Place a layer of lightweight tear-away stabilizer under the edge to prevent puckering, and stitch just inside the edge. Remove the stabilizer and carefully trim the fabric close to the stitching.

2. Sew an 8-inch-long strip to each long strip: press the seams open or serge together with a narrow overlock stitch.

3. Arrange the strips in four rows so the seams alternate as shown in Figure 1 on page 104. This way the seams won't all show up on the same side of the finished bag; the seams will be less obvious or visible. Finish the lower edge of each strip with a tiny zigzag stitch or a narrow rolled hem on the serger. Use rayon thread in the upper looper of the serger and a longer-than-normal stitch for the rolled edge to keep the edges fluid. Use stabilizer as needed to control puckering. Trim zigzagged edges if necessary.

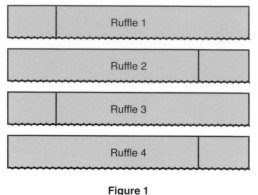

Figure 1
Finish lower edge of each ruffle strip.

4. With right sides together, sew the short ends of each scarf strip together using a ½-inch-wide seam allowance; press the seams open. Machine-baste ½ inch from the upper edge of each scarf circle, beginning and ending the stitching at the seam line. Mark the center of the strip opposite the seam allowance.

5. Sew the short ends of each solid-fabric strip together; press and mark the center as for the scarf strips.

6. With the wrong side of a ruffle strip on the right side of solid-fabric row 1 strip, match the seams and centers and pin. Draw up the basting to fit and adjust the gathers evenly. Pin and stitch ½ inch from the raw edges. Set aside (Figure 2).

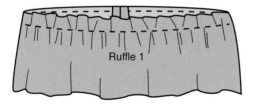

Figure 2
Sew each ruffle to the right side of
its corresponding fabric strip.

7. Repeat step 6 with each of the remaining scarf and solid strips.

8. Arrange the ruffled strips in order. With seams matching, pin the lower edge of strip 1 to the upper edge of strip 2, keeping the lower edge of ruffle 1 out of the seam; stitch.

9. Sew the remaining ruffled circles to the solid-fabric strips in order. Zigzag-finish the raw edges of each seam together and press the seams toward strip 4.

10. Fold the ruffled panel in half with the seam centered; pin. Lightly press the two folded edges to mark the sides. Stitch ¼ inch from the lower raw edges, taking care to keep the ruffle edge out of the seam; press the seam open (Figure 3).

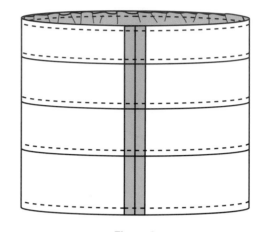

Figure 3
Stitch the ruffle panels together in order to create the bag body.
Keep the lower edge of each ruffle out of the way of the stitching.

11. With right sides together, align the bottom seam line with a side crease and draw a line ¾ inch from the point at the corner. Stitch on the line, backstitching at the beginning and end of the stitching. Stitch again ⅛ inch from the first stitching and trim the point close to the stitching (Figure 4). Repeat at the opposite side to box the bag bottom. Turn the bag right side out.

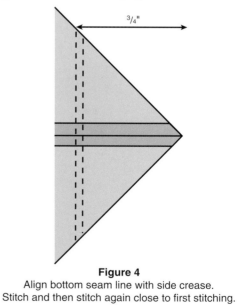

Figure 4
Align bottom seam line with side crease.
Stitch and then stitch again close to first stitching.

12. Apply a light coat of temporary spray adhesive to the wrong side of the two lining rectangles and smooth them in place on the 11 x 24-inch piece of fleece. Cut along the lining edges and discard excess fleece. Using a marking pen, draw lines on the fleece 1 inch from the upper edge and ¼ inch from the side and bottom edges. Lift the fleece edges from the lining and cut away the fleece along the lines. Smooth the fleece back in place on the lining. This eliminates bulk in the seams.

13. Draw a 1¼-inch-diagonal grid on the fleece and machine-stitch on each line to quilt the layers together. Apply fabric protector to the lining side.

14. From lining fabric scraps, cut a 1 x 4-inch strip. Fold in half lengthwise with wrong sides together and press. Turn the raw edges into the fold and press. Stitch close to both long edges. Cut into two equal lengths. Loop each strip through an O ring and baste the raw edges together. Position the strips at the side seam edges of one lining piece 1½ inches below the upper edge; machine-baste in place (Figure 5).

Note: *If you use a chain strap recycled from a thrift store bag, it may already have O rings attached.*

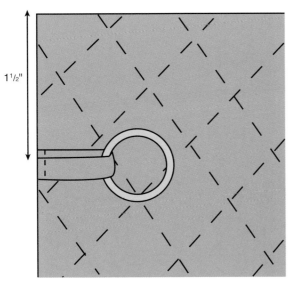

1½"

Figure 5
Sew O-ring loops to side-seam
edges of quilted lining panel.

15. With right sides together, sew the two lining pieces together at the side and bottom edges using ¼-inch-wide seams. If you have your own designer label, stitch it now to the right side of one lining piece. Box the bottom corners as shown in Figure 4, but stitch only ⅝ inch from the points. The finished lining will be slightly smaller than the bag so it will fit more smoothly into the corners.

16. With wrong sides together, insert the lining into the ruffled bag. With your hand inside the bag, adjust the lining so that the corners are aligned and the sides are smooth. Pin the upper edge of the bag to the lining with the upper 1 inch of the lining extending above the bag upper edge.

17. To reinforce the snap closure, cut two 1 x 1½-inch pieces of milk-jug plastic. Using one perforated metal disk of the magnetic snap set, mark and cut two vertical slits on each plastic piece. Again using the perforated disk, mark and cut two vertical slits in the right side of the lining back, 1 inch from the upper edge. Insert the prongs of the socket half of the snap into the slits, and on the fleece side, position the perforated disk and the plastic piece over the prongs. Bend the prongs toward the outer edges of the bag (Figure 6). Apply the other half of the snap to the opposite half of the lining.

Milk-jug plastic

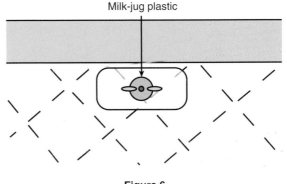

Figure 6
Apply magnetic snaps to quilted lining on inside.

18. Turn under and press a scant ⅛ inch around the upper edge of the lining. Turn the lining down over the upper edge of the bag and slipstitch in place.

19. Optional: *Sew teardrop beads to the ruffle edges if desired, evenly spacing eight beads along each edge (see bag photo on page 103).*

20. Create a tassel using the buttons and some unusual finds. The one shown was made from an old button from a thrift-store coat, a metal earring shaped in a Chinese character (meaning "luck"), a small chain from a broken necklace, and a carved stone amulet purchased at a bead store. To make a charm like this, first attach a sturdy O ring through the button shank to provide something to hang the "charms" from. Then suspend your charms with jump rings, and hang the tassel using the necklace chain looped through the O ring (I also threaded the chain through the carved amulet for added Asian flair). Finally, stitch the button with dangling charms to the bag front, and reinforce it with a small button inside the bag.

21. Use small jump rings to attach the chain handle to the O rings inside the bag. ●

Hankies Will Do

You can use old hankies to make a similar bag. Because they are much smaller, you'll need at least six of them for a bag similar to the one shown. Search for them in your favorite colors at thrift and vintage clothing stores. Instead of cutting the hankies into strips and sewing them to strips of base fabric, use the following method to create a similar tiered effect.

1. Arrange the hankies on the surface of a completed outer shell so their corners point downward, and stagger them like roof shingles around the entire bag circumference.

2. When satisfied with the arrangement, trim each hankie to fit, then finish the cut edges.

3. Instead of gathering each hankie "shingle," simply hand-stitch the upper edge of each one to the bag surface.

4. Complete your bag as directed.

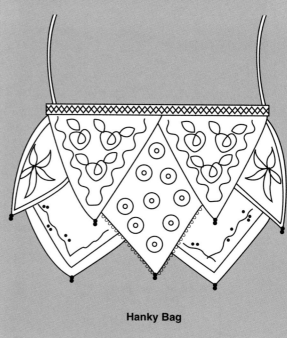

Hanky Bag

HARLEQUIN ROMANCE

DESIGN BY JANIS BULLIS

You won't go unnoticed when you carry this roomy and colorful bag. Quilted cotton velveteen is the perfect backdrop for beaded accents and feather trim.

INSTRUCTIONS

Project Notes: *Use ½-inch-wide seam allowances throughout. Read Handling Velveteen on page 111 before proceeding.*

• Enlarge the bag pattern pieces (Figure 1) on pattern tracing paper and cut out. Trace the diamond onto template plastic and cut out using rotary-cutting tools.

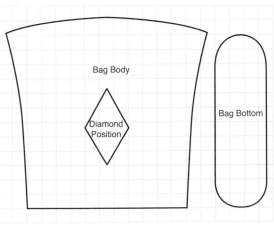

Figure 1
Bag Pattern
1 square = 1"

FINISHED SIZE

11 x 12 x 2½ inches

MATERIALS

• ⅝ yard black cotton velveteen
• ⅞ yard printed satin for lining
• 1 yard 20-inch-wide heavy-weight double-sided fusible nonwoven stabilizer (Fast2Fuse)
• 5 x 10-inch rectangle medium-weight fusible interfacing
• ½ yard ⅞-inch-diameter cotton filler cord
• All-purpose thread to match or contrast with fabrics and beads
• Pattern tracing paper or cloth
• Template plastic
• 32-inch-long piece feather boa trim
• 6 (⅜-inch-long) round beads or buttons
• 24 (¾-inch-long) teardrop beads
• 24 (½-inch-diameter) teardrop beads
• 1 large snap or 1 square of hook-and-loop tape
• Pencil
• Air-soluble marking pen or white tailor's chalk
• Rotary cutter, mat and ruler
• Basic sewing tools and equipment

- From the velveteen, cut two bag bodies and one bag bottom. Using rotary-cutting tools, cut two 3½ x 12¼-inch rectangles for the bag sides and one 3½ x 12¼-inch strip for the handle.
- From the lining, cut two bag bodies, one bag bottom, two 3½ x 12¼-inch rectangles for the sides, one 5 x 10-inch pocket rectangle and six 1 x 14-inch true-bias strips for finishing the seam edges on the inside of the bag.
- From the heavy fusible nonwoven stabilizer, cut two bag bodies and one bag bottom. Trim ½ inch from all edges of each piece. For the side panels, cut two 2½ x 11¼-inch pieces.

Assembly

1. Apply the 5 x 10-inch rectangle of fusible interfacing to the wrong side of the lining pocket rectangle following the manufacturer's directions. Fold the lining pocket rectangle in half crosswise with raw edges even. Stitch ½ inch from all raw edges, leaving a 3-inch opening in the lower edge for turning. Trim the seams to ¼ inch. Turn the pocket right side out and press, turning in the opening edges. Position the pocket on the right side of one lining piece 3 inches below the upper curved edge. Stitch the side and bottom edges in place (Figure 2).

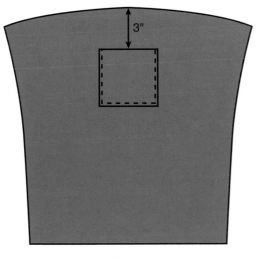

Figure 2
Sew pocket to bag lining.

2. With right sides together, stitch the upper curved edge of the remaining lining piece to one of the velveteen bag pieces. Trim the seam to ¼ inch, press the

seam open over a pressing ham and then turn the lining to the inside and press the upper edge.

3. Position a piece of the fusible heavyweight fusible stabilizer on the wrong side of the bag under the lining with ½ inch of the bag extending beyond the side and bottom edges of the stabilizer (Figure 3). Smooth the lining in place on top. Fuse following the manufacturer's directions. Stitch close to the upper finished edge of the completed piece. Machine-baste ⅜ inch from the raw edges.

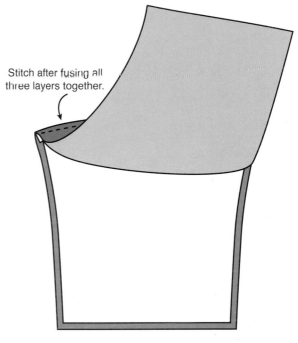

Stitch after fusing all three layers together.

Figure 3
Position fusible stabilizer on bag fron wrong side.

4. Repeat steps 2 and 3 with the remaining bag body and the lining piece with the pocket. In the same manner, sew the side lining rectangles to the velveteen rectangles at the upper edge. Trim and press, add the stabilizer between the velvet and lining layers and fuse. Set the side panels and the panel with the pocket aside.

5. On the remaining bag panel, draw the diamond quilting grid on the velveteen using an air-soluble marking pen or tailor's chalk. Use the diamond template as a guide for spacing the lines and creating the correct angle. Using a contrasting-color thread, stitch on the lines to quilt the bag front. Tie off all threads neatly on the lining side at the upper edge of the bag (Figure 4 on page 110).

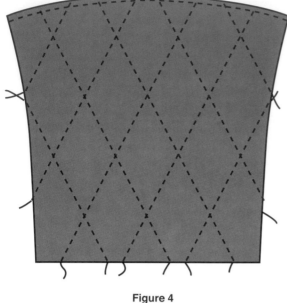

Figure 4
Quilt bag front to lining.

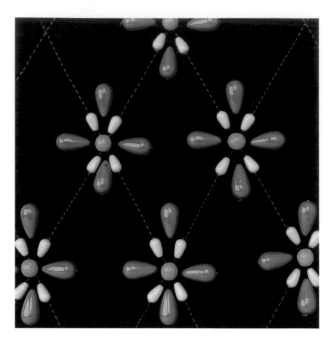

6. Refer to the photo to position and sew beads in place, beginning with the round beads at the grid-line intersections.

7. With right sides together, sew the bag side panels to the bag front and back panels. Trim the seam allowances to ¼ inch and finish by binding the layers together at each seam with one of the bias strips (Figure 5).

Note: *If you prefer, finish the seams with closely spaced serging in a color to match the lining fabric.*

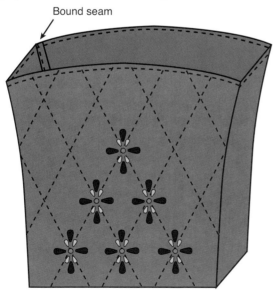

Figure 5
Sew bag side to front and back. Bind seams inside bag.

8. Fold the bag bottom piece in half crosswise and snip-mark the center fold at each raw edge. Fold in half lengthwise and snip-mark the fold at each end. Sandwich the bag bottom stabilizer between the velveteen and lining bottom pieces and fuse the layers together as you did for the bag and side pieces.

9. Mark the center at the bottom edge of the bag front and back, and the center of each side panel. With right sides facing and centers matching, pin the bottom panel to the bag. Clip as shown in Figure 6 to fit the bag smoothly around the curved ends of the bottom panel. Stitch. Trim the seam to ¼ inch.

Figure 6
Sew bag bottom to bag.

10. Sew the remaining bias strips together using a ¼-inch-wide seam allowance and press the seam open. Use the strip to bind the bottom seam (or serge-finish instead).

11. Fold the velveteen strip for the handle in half lengthwise with right sides facing and stitch ½ inch from the raw edges. Turn right side out.

12. Machine-stitch a long piece of heavy cord to one end of the filler cord. Thread the heavy cord into a bodkin and use it to pull the cord through the velveteen tube for the handle. Allow the fabric to gather over the cord, leaving ½ inch of the fabric tube ungathered at each end. Hand-tack the fabric to the filler cord at each end of the gathers (not at the raw edges). Turn the raw edges into the tube at each end and machine-stitch together. Position the ends on the inside of the bag at each side panel and machine-stitch in place. Distribute gathers evenly along the filler cord.

13. Sew the snap in place at the top edge on the inside of the bag.

14. Hand-sew the feather boa to the upper edge of the bag. ●

Template

Diamond Quilting Template
Actual Size

Handling Velveteen

Velveteen is a napped fabric and requires some special handling.

• Cut all pieces with the nap running in the same direction to avoid obvious differences in color shading.

• Use a special pressing board designed to protect the nap. Velvet needleboards have small spikes that the nap can nestle into when pressing so you don't flatten the pile with the weight of the iron.

• If available, use a walking foot or engage the even-feed feature on your machine to keep the layers from shifting while stitching.

LITTLE LUXURY

DESIGN BY KAREN DILLON

Combine bits of velvet, brocade and taffeta for a luxurious little evening bag. Tuck your essentials inside for a special night out on the town.

INSTRUCTIONS

Cutting
- From the taffeta, cut one 3½ x 26-inch rectangle and two 6½ x 7½-inch rectangles.
- From the velvet, cut two 6 x 7½-inch pieces.
- From the brocade, cut two 2½ x 6½-inch strips.
- Enlarge the pattern for the bag (Figure 1) on pattern tracing paper or tissue and cut out. Use it to cut two pieces from the lining.
- From the flannel interlining, cut two 7½ x 11½-inch rectangles.

FINISHED SIZE
7 x 10 inches, excluding straps

Project Note: *All seam allowances are ¼ inch wide.*

MATERIALS
- ⅜ yard taffeta
- 6 x 16-inch piece velvet
- 6 x 8-inch scrap metallic brocade
- ¼ yard lining
- ¼ yard beaded trim
- ½ yard narrow decorative cord
- 1¼ yards 1¼-inch-diameter twisted cord for strap
- 2 (8 x 12-inch) rectangles of cotton flannel for interlining
- 1 small decorative button
- Pattern tracing paper or tissue
- All-purpose thread to match fabrics
- Rotary cutter, mat and ruler
- Press cloth
- Point turner
- Basic sewing tools and equipment

Assembly

1. Working on a soft surface you can pin into, make random tapered tucks across the width of the 26-inch-long strip of taffeta. Pin tucks to the pinning surface as you make them and fold them from opposite edges so the wide ends of the uneven tucks alternate (Figure 2). Pleat the strip down to 6½ inches in length. Carefully readjust the pins so you can remove the piece from the pinning surface and stitch ⅛ inch from the long edges.

2. Center the pleated panel on one 6½ x 7½-inch taffeta rectangle. Pin in place. With right sides facing, pin a brocade strip to one long edge of the pleated panel.

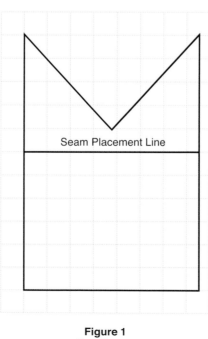

Figure 1
Bag Pattern
1 square = 1"

Seam Placement Line

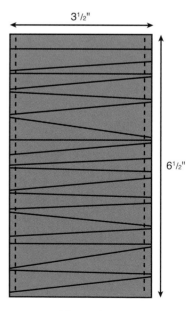

3¹/₂"

6¹/₂"

Figure 2
Make uneven pleats across width of strip.

Stitch ¼ inch from the long edges. Flip the brocade away from the pleats and press, using a press cloth to protect the fabrics (Figure 3). Do not press the pleats flat.

3. Add the remaining brocade strip to the opposite edge in the same manner. Machine-baste ⅛ inch from the long outer edges.

4. Cut two 6½-inch-long pieces of the narrow decorative cord and position them in the seam lines. Adjust the machine for a narrow zigzag stitch and couch the cords in place.

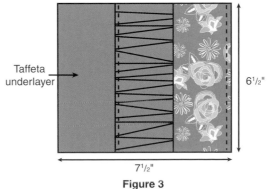

Taffeta underlayer

6½"

7½"

Figure 3
Sew pleated and brocade panels to right side of taffeta rectangle.

5. With right sides facing, pin one piece of velvet to the upper edge of the brocade/pleated panel. Stitch ¼ inch from the raw edges. Hold the steam iron above the piece and use your fingers to press the seam toward the velvet. Sew the remaining piece of velvet to the upper edge of the remaining 6½ x 7½-inch rectangle and press in the same manner (Figure 4).

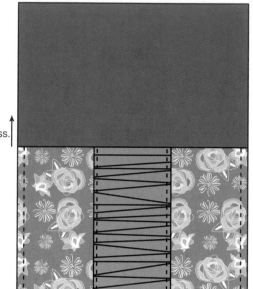

Figure 4
Sew velvet to lower panel.

6. Place a flannel rectangle on the wrong side of each bag piece and pin in place. Place the bag pattern piece on top of each panel and pin in place with the placement line along the seam line. Cut out and then machine-baste ⅛ inch from all raw edges of each piece.

7. Cut a 7-inch-long piece of beaded trim and center it between the ¼-inch seam allowances at the lower edge of one of the bag pieces. Align the upper edge of the trim header with the lower raw edge of the bag, with the beaded fringe lying on the right side of the bag, pointing to the upper edge. Make sure the beads do not extend into the ¼-inch seam allowances at each side of the bag.

8. With right sides facing, sew the bag front and back together along the side and bottom edges. Press the side seams open over a point turner. Sew the lining pieces together in the same manner, leaving a 4-inch opening in the bottom seam for turning. Do not turn the lining right side out.

9. With raw edges even, pin the cord ends of the strap to the upper edges of the bag at the side seams. Check the cord length and adjust as needed. As cut, it is long enough to wear with the strap over your head so it crosses your chest. If that is too long, shorten the strap or tie the ends in an adjustable overhand knot. Baste the cord ends in place.

10. Tuck the bag inside the lining with upper raw edges even; stitch. When you are about 1 inch from a center front or back point, shorten the stitch length and continue. At the point, pivot and stitch one or two small stitches, pivot again, stitch for an inch and then return to the normal stitch length until you are within 1 inch of the other point. Stitch and pivot in the same manner to complete the stitching (Figure 5).

Figure 5
Sew lining to bag upper edge.

11. Carefully turn the bag right side out through the opening in the lining. Turn under and press the opening edges in the lining and stitch them together. Tuck the lining into the bag and finger-press the upper edges with the help of a little steam from the iron. To keep the lining from rolling out at the upper edge, hand-stitch the lining to the seam allowance only. Tack the lining to the bag at the side seams. ●

ALL BUTTONED UP

DESIGN BY PAM LINDQUIST

The Pearlies of London would love this little evening bag. (These legendary costermongers—now entertainers— still dress in clothing embellished in pearl buttons; check at your local library or research them on the World Wide Web). The bag is the perfect size for only the necessary items you might need for an evening out.

INSTRUCTIONS

Project Note:
Use ¼-inch-wide seam allowances throughout.

Cutting

- Cut a 9 x 20-inch piece of interfacing and fuse to the wrong side of the bag fabric following the manufacturer's directions.
- Enlarge the bag pattern (Figure 1) on pattern tracing paper or cloth and cut out. Use the pattern to cut two bag pieces each from the interfaced fabric and the lining. Cut one bag shape from the remaining interfacing and apply to the interfaced side of one of the bag pieces (bag back) so it has a double layer of interfacing.
- From the remaining uninterfaced bag fabric, cut two 1¼ x 22-inch strips for wrapping the bangles.

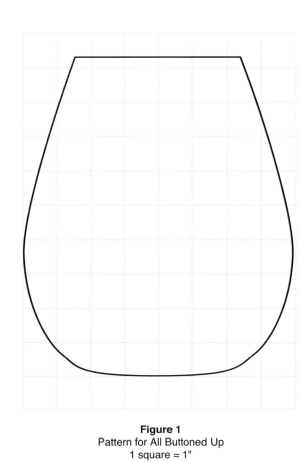

Figure 1
Pattern for All Buttoned Up
1 square = 1"

FINISHED SIZE

7 x 8 inches, excluding the handles

MATERIALS

- ⅜ yard silk dupioni or other fabric for bag body
- ⅜ yard lining
- ⅜ yard light- to medium-weight fusible weft-insertion interfacing
- All-purpose thread to match fabrics
- 9 x 10-inch piece of pattern tracing paper or cloth
- Air- or water-soluble marking pen
- Assorted white shell buttons, ¼–¾ inch in diameter
- 2 bangle bracelets (approximately ¼ inch thick) for bag handles
- Point turner for pressing
- Basic sewing tools and equipment

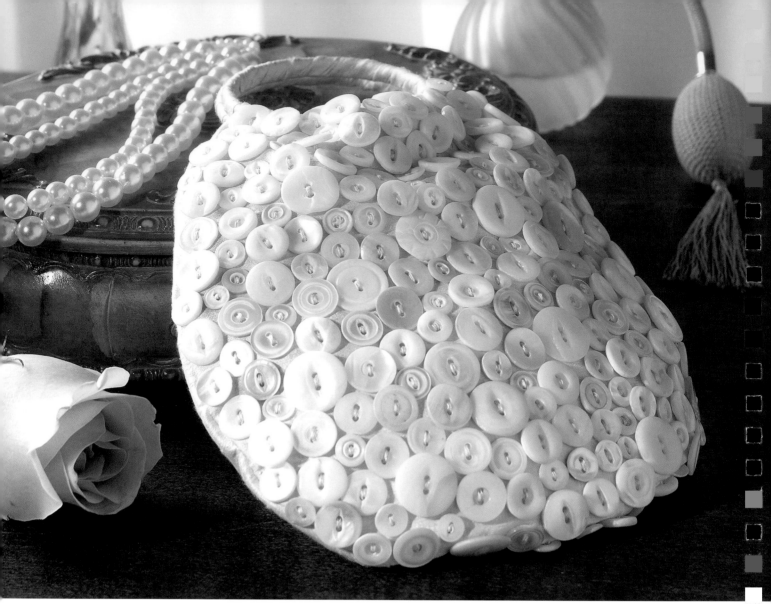

Assembly

1. On each bag and lining piece, machine-stitch a scant ¼ inch from the raw edges, beginning at the upper edge and continuing for a total of 5 inches from the upper edge (Figure 2).

2. With right sides together, sew a lining piece to each bag piece, ending the stitching 3⅜ inches from the upper edge on each side. Clip the seam allowance at the end of the stitching

(Figure 3). Slip the pieces over a point turner and press the seams open.

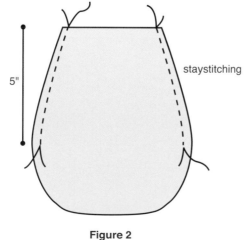

Figure 2
Staystitch side seams of bag pieces.

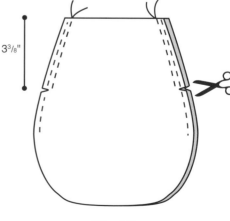

Figure 3
Stitch lining to bag piece just inside staystitching. Clip to stitching.

3. With right sides together, pin the bag pieces together and the lining pieces together. Stitch the pieces together (Figure 4). Turn right side out through the opening at the upper edge of the bag. Press as needed. Stitch the lining to the bag a scant ¼ inch from each upper raw edge.

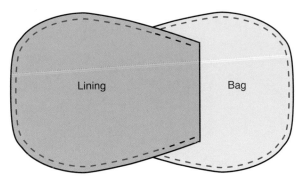

Figure 4
Sew linings together, beginning and ending at clips. Repeat with bag.

4. Arrange and sew the buttons to the bag front. Allow as little or as much of the bag fabric to show around the buttons and sew them in place through the bag layer only—not the lining. Buttons must end 1½ inches from the unfinished upper edge of the bag front (Figure 5).

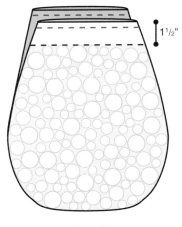

1½"

Figure 5
Sew buttons to bag front, ending them 1½" from the upper edge.

5. Turn under and press ¼ inch at each long edge of the fabric strips for the handles. Use the strips to wrap each bangle with fabric, overlapping the strips at an angle as you wrap. Cut away any excess strip and sew (or glue) the strip end in place.

6. Turn under and press ¼ inch at each upper edge of the bag, using the stitching as a guide. With the raw end of the strip on the wrapped bangle toward the bottom of

the bag, wrap the bag edge over a bangle and slipstitch the inner edge securely in place (Figure 6). Repeat with the remaining handle. ●

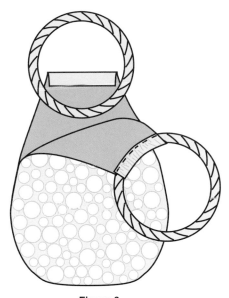

Figure 6
Wrap upper edges over bangles and slipstitch in place.

Jewel It!

For an entirely different look, use hot-fix jewels or crystals to embellish a printed cotton bag. You can embellish both sides of the bag with these lightweight jewels. Use decorative bangle bracelets for the handles instead of wrapping bangles with fabric.

For a larger bag, enlarge the pattern as desired and use readymade handles. Another option for a handle on larger bags is to wrap embroidery hoops with fabric strips or ribbon as shown for the "Pearlie" bag.

SOMETHING BORROWED, SOMETHING BLUE

DESIGN BY HOPE YODER

Create a cherished heirloom for a favorite bride. She can use this sweet little bag as her "something blue" and then pass it on to a friend or daughter someday to use as "something borrowed." Heirloom stitching transforms a bit of linen into this distinctly feminine treasure.

FINISHED SIZE

5½ x 5½ inches, excluding strap

MATERIALS

- 2 (9-inch) squares blue handkerchief linen (heavily starched)
- 5 x 7-inch and 5 x 12-inch pieces of white silk organza
- 2-inch-long white tassel
- Lightweight tear-away stabilizer
- Water-soluble marking pen
- 12-weight cotton thread
- Size 120 wing needle
- Size 80 Microtex needle
- Size 100 sewing machine needle
- Open-toe presser foot
- Gimp or entredeux presser foot (or substitute a cording foot)
- 40-weight rayon thread to match the linen
- 45 inches of white gimp cord or #6 pearl crown thread
- Double-eyed hand-sewing needle
- Gold metallic thread
- Husqvarna Viking Embroidery Card #9 or other monogram design of your choice
- 7-inch square of transparent acetate for cutting template
- 2 (3 x 7-inch) pieces of heavyweight water-soluble stabilizer
- Clear acrylic ruler
- Paper-backed fusible web
- Point turner
- Fine glass-head pins
- Basic sewing tools and equipment

INSTRUCTIONS

Assembly

1. Using a water-soluble marking pen, draw a line through the center of one 9-inch square of starched linen. Draw three lines on each side of the center, spacing them ¾ inch apart.

2. Refer to Figure 1 for steps 2 and 3. Fold both pieces of silk organza in half lengthwise and press. Use a water-soluble marking pen to mark fold lines on the longer of the two folded pieces as shown in Figure 1.

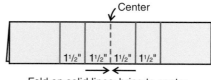

Fold on solid lines; bring to center.
Fold on remaining lines to make ³⁄₈-inch-wide pleats.

Figure 1
Mark silk for pleating.

Note: *Make an actual-size paper template and apply the folded silk to it with temporary spray adhesive to make it easier to mark.*

3. Pleat the fabric toward the center on both sides. Note that the outermost pleats lie on top of the inner pleats. Press. Machine-baste ¼ inch from the upper and lower edges of the pleated strip to keep the pleats in place while you work. Set the organza strips aside.

4. Insert the size 120 wing needle in the sewing machine and thread with lightweight white thread in the needle and bobbin. Select the built-in hemstitch or wide entredeux stitch (Figure 2). Adjust the stitch to 4.5mm long and 4.0mm wide.

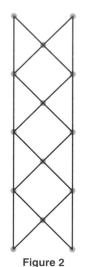

Figure 2
Entredeux Stitch

5. Place a layer of lightweight tear-away stabilizer on the wrong side of the fabric to support the work. Stitch over the centerline on the marked linen square. Repeat on each of the second lines to the right and left of the center. Every other row will have wing-needle stitching.

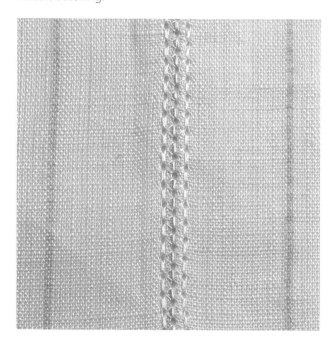

6. Replace the entredeux needle with the size 80 Microtex needle. Use lightweight thread in the bobbin

and 40-weight rayon thread in the needle. It should match the fabric color.

7. Adjust the machine for a satin stitch (2mm wide and 3mm long). The stabilizer should still be on the wrong side of the piece of linen. Insert the gimp cord into the slot on the gimp or entredeux presser foot.

8. Test the stitching first on scraps of linen and stabilizer before stitching on the linen to make sure the satin stitch completely covers the cord. Adjust the stitch settings as needed. Stitch over the gimp along each of the remaining lines on the linen. Center the presser foot over the lines and begin stitching while holding the cord along the line. Carefully remove the stabilizer from the back of the piece.

9. Thread gold metallic thread through one end of the double-eyed needle and do a running stitch through the center of each row of entredeux. The stitches should go over two holes and under one so the stitches on the front are longer than the stitches on the back.

10. Apply a light coat of spray starch to the wrong side of the linen square and press to remove wrinkles.

11. Fold the stitched linen square in half crosswise and crease to mark the center for the machine embroidery. Hoop one layer of tear-away stabilizer and then draw vertical and horizontal placement lines on the hooped stabilizer using a water-soluble marking pen.

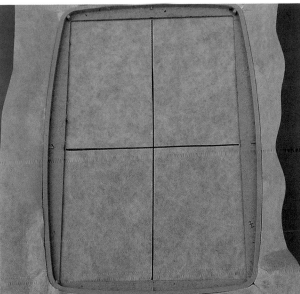

12. Apply a light coat of temporary adhesive to the marked side of the stabilizer. Smooth the linen piece on top, aligning the centerlines on the fabric with the centerlines on the stabilizer.

Note: *This method of hooping prevents hoop burn and distortion on delicate fabrics.*

13. Choose the desired monogram embroidery design that is about 1½ inches tall and wide. Download to the embroidery unit and embroider it in the center of the fabric. Unhoop the stabilizer and carefully remove it from the fabric. Place the embroidery face down on a padded surface and press lightly.

14. Trace the bag pattern on page 123 onto the acetate square and mark the embroidery placement cross lines. Cut out the acetate pattern.

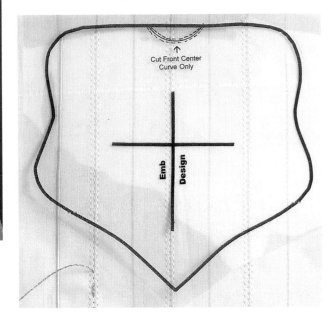

15. Position the pattern on the embroidered panel, centering it on the centerline. Draw around the outer edge to mark the cutting line. Remove the transparency and cut out the front panel, cutting along the curved line at the upper edge of the center front. Repeat for the back, but cut straight across the upper edge.

16. Set up the machine with the Microtex needle, using lightweight thread in the needle and on the bobbin. Adjust for a 1.5mm stitch length. Place a strip of the water-soluble stabilizer across the upper edge on the right side of each piece of linen with about ½ inch of excess extending at each side. Stitch ¼ inch from the upper edge of the purse front and back. Trim the stabilizer even with the upper and side edge, and clip the curve on the bag front. Turn the stabilizer to the wrong side of the piece like you would a facing; finger-press in place. Use a point turner to smooth out the curved area as needed. Press lightly from the right side only. Do not touch stabilizer with the iron.

17. Slip the raw edges of the pleated silk strip under the upper edge of the front bag piece, matching centers. Repeat with the raw edges of the unpleated silk strip and the back bag piece. Adjust so 1 inch of the silk extends above the edge at each side. Pin in place. Tuck a small piece of narrow fusible web between the bag and strip under the curved area on the bag front, and fuse the layers together to keep the curve in place for stitching.

18. Insert the size 100 needle and use lightweight white thread in the needle and on the bobbin. Select a pin stitch or one that looks like the one shown in Figure 3 and adjust for a 2.0mm stitch length and a stitch width of 2.5mm.

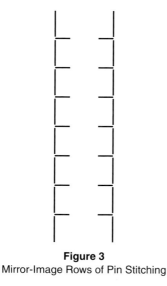

Figure 3
Mirror-Image Rows of Pin Stitching

19. Stitch along the edge of the linen with the vertical stitches in the organza and the horizontal stitches in the linen. You may need to use the mirror-image function on your machine to position the stitch correctly. Stop with the needle down at the center of the curve and raise the foot to adjust for a smooth turn.

20. For the second row of stitching, sew through all layers ¼ inch from the first stitching with horizontal stitches pointing to the upper edge of the bag. Repeat on the bag back.

21. With right sides together, stitch the bag front to the back ¼ inch from the raw edges. Use an overcasting stitch and adjust it for a length of 1.5mm and width of 5mm. **Note:** *To make it easy to attach the tassel at the bottom, leave a small opening at the bottom point of the purse.* Stop sewing and tie off the stitches about ⅛ inch from the bottom point. Begin stitching again ⅛ inch from the point on the remaining half of the bag. This leaves a small hole through which to pull the tassel cord. Press seams flat and turn the bag right side out, using a point turner to smooth out the curves.

22. To attach the tassel, thread a hand-sewing needle with matching thread and loop it through the tassel loop. Knot the thread ends together. From the right side of the bag, insert the needle in the small hole at the point of the bag and pull it up through the purse. Tug gently to pull the tassel loop into the bag. Secure the tassel by turning the purse wrong side out and stitch the cord to the seam allowance.

23. To make the twisted cord handle, cut 15 pieces of thread, each 40 inches long, in coordinating colors. Use

some heavier threads such as 12-weight and metallic threads. From the back, place the threads and cords through the center of an empty bobbin and place the spool on the bobbin winder with the thread ends positioned so you can grasp them. If the bobbin will not slip easily onto the spindle, remove a few threads so that it will. Ask someone to hold the thread ends taut behind you while you hold onto the tails coming out from the underside of the bobbin. Press on the foot pedal as if you were winding a bobbin and run the machine until the threads are tightly twisted. Remove the bobbin from the spindle without letting go of either end of the twisted threads. Bring both cut ends of the twisted thread

together and allow the two halves of the cord to twist together. Smooth out any kinks and tie a knot at the ends to secure the twist.

24. Hand-sew the handle to the inside of the purse at the side seams.

25. *Optional:* *Embellish the completed bag with crystals or beads by hand or try the L'orna Decorative Touch Wand to attach hot-fix crystals.*

26. Use a dampened cloth to remove any markings that show on the organza or the bag. ●

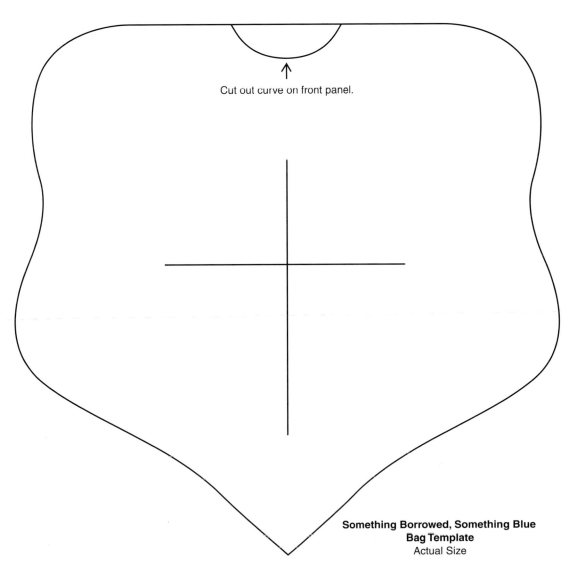

Cut out curve on front panel.

**Something Borrowed, Something Blue
Bag Template**
Actual Size

MAKE IT MANDARIN

DESIGN BY ANNETTE BAILEY

Simple cutting and sewing turns a pretty piece of brocade into a Mandarin-collared bag. Chinese knot buttons and a braided drapery tieback complete this easy-to-sew bag.

FINISHED SIZE

9 x 12 inches, excluding handle and trim

MATERIALS

- ³⁄₈ yard oriental print brocade (see Note below)
- ³⁄₈ yard lining fabric
- ³⁄₈ yard of light- to medium-weight fusible interfacing
- 3 (⁵⁄₈-inch-diameter) Chinese ball knot buttons or small frog closures to coordinate with fabric
- All-purpose thread to match fabrics
- ¹⁄₃ yard beaded trim
- 1 drapery tieback for the handle
- Press cloth
- Basic sewing tools and equipment

Note: *You will have extra fabric for a matching eyeglass case (see For Your Eyes Only on page 127), plus some to tuck away for other projects. This yardage allows for cutting the bag piece with the longest dimension along the fabric width and the shortest dimension parallel to the selvages.*

INSTRUCTIONS

Cutting

- From the brocade and from the fusible interfacing, cut one 13 x 20-inch rectangle and one 3 x 18-inch strip for the collar. Apply the interfacing to the wrong side of each strip following the manufacturer's directions.
- From the lining fabric, cut one 13 x 20-inch rectangle.

Optional: *Apply a matching piece of interfacing to the lining to add body and longer wear to the finished bag.*

Assembly

1. Fold the brocade rectangle in half crosswise with short raw edges even. Stitch ½ inch from the raw edges and press the seam open.

2. Turn right side out and center the seam on the back layer of the bag. Mark the position of the seam on the back layer with snip marks at the upper and lower edges. Also snip-mark the fold at

the sides. Baste the header of the beaded trim to the lower edge on the front of the bag only. Position the lower edge of the trim header at the ½-inch seam line from snip mark to snip mark on the bag front. Machine-baste in place, using a zipper foot so you can stitch close to the trim if necessary (Figure 1).

Snip.

Snip centers and folds.

Figure 1
Baste beaded trim to lower front edge.

Note: Alternatively, you can create your own beaded trim and sew it to the bottom edge of the finished bag after completing step 8.

3. Turn the bag wrong side out. With the seam line centered at the snip mark on the back layer of the bag, stitch ½ inch from the bottom raw edges. Stitch from the front of the bag so you can follow the basting for the trim and stitch just inside it. Turn right side out and press the bottom edge, using a press cloth to protect the fabric and trim as needed.

4. With wrong sides facing, fold the collar strip in half lengthwise. Stitch ½ inch from the short ends. Trim the seams to ¼ inch, clip the corners, turn and press.

5. With the short ends of the strip ½ inch from the center front seam, pin the collar to the upper edge of the bag. Stitch ⅜ inch from the raw edges through all layers (Figure 2).

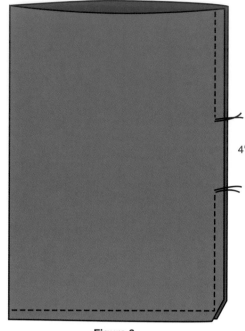

Figure 3
Leave opening in lining.

Figure 2
Baste collar to upper edge.

6. Fold the lining panel in half crosswise with right sides together and stitch ½ inch from the side and bottom raw edges. Leave a 4-inch-long opening in the longer seam for turning (Figure 3). Clip the corner and press the seams to one side.

7. Tuck the bag into the lining with right sides together. Stitch ½ inch from the upper edge. Turn the bag right side out through the opening in the lining. Machine-stitch the opening edges closed.

8. Position the buttons (or frog closures) along the center front seam as desired, spacing them 2½ or 3 inches apart. Sew in place, catching the lining in the stitches.

9. Securely hand-sew the ends of the drapery tieback for the handle to the inside of the bag. ●

For Your Eyes Only

Make a matching eyeglass case from fabric scraps—or make a smaller, similar case for your cell phone using the same method outlined here.

1. From brocade and lining fabric, cut a 4 x 18-inch rectangle. From lightweight batting, cut a 4 x 14-inch strip.

2. Position the batting on the wrong side of the brocade with short and long edges even; turn under and press ¼ inch at the short end without the batting. Fold the brocade end back onto the right side of the batting-backed brocade with 4¼ inches of brocade extending above the short, turned edge. Stitch ¼ inch from the long raw edges through all layers (Figure 1). Clip across the corners. Turn right side out. Repeat with the lining, but do not turn right side out.

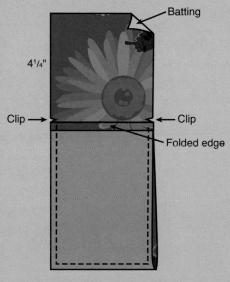

Figure 1
Fold and stitch.

3. Tuck the brocade case into the lining and pin with raw edges even. Stitch the brocade and lining flaps together ¼ inch from the raw edges, ending and backstitching at the turned opening edges. Clip across the corners (Figure 2).

Figure 2
Stitch lining to flap, ending the stitching at the folded edge of the case.

4. Turn the case and lining right side out through the opening. Tuck the lining inside the case. Slipstitch the turned opening edges together.

5. Make a buttonhole in the flap and sew a button (or decorative frog closure) in place underneath.

BEA-DAZZLED

DESIGN BY MARTA ALTO

Clusters of beads dance on the surface of this silken drawstring bag. Ready-made beaded fringe trim is easy to apply. If you are a beader, you can customize this design with your own beaded tassels.

INSTRUCTIONS

Project Note: *Use ¼-inch-wide seam allowances unless otherwise directed.*

FINISHED SIZE

9½ x 9 x 2½ inches, excluding loops and strap

MATERIALS

- ½ yard 45-inch-wide silk dupioni or other similar-weight fabric for bag
- ½ yard 45-inch-wide lining fabric
- ½ yard beaded fringe trim
- 1½ yards decorative cord for strap
- ½ yard medium-weight fusible weft-insertion interfacing
- ½ yard lightweight fusible weft-insertion interfacing
- ⅜ yard thin cotton batting
- Optional: temporary spray adhesive
- Masking tape
- All-purpose thread to match fabrics
- Rotary cutter, mat and ruler
- Basic sewing tools and equipment

Cutting

- From the silk dupioni, the lining and the medium-weight interfacing, cut two 10-inch squares for the bag front and back and three 3 x 10-inch strips for the sides and bottom. Apply the interfacing to the wrong side of each piece following the manufacturer's directions.
- Repeat the above with the lining fabric and the lightweight fusible interfacing.
- From the batting, cut two 10-inch squares and three 3 x 10-inch strips.
- From the remaining silk and lightweight fusible interfacing, cut two 1½ x 19-inch strips for the loops. Apply the interfacing to the wrong side of each strip.
- From the remaining lining, cut one 7½ x 9-inch and one 4 x 9-inch pocket rectangle. Back each one with a matching piece of lightweight fusible interfacing following the manufacturer's directions.

Assembly

1. Pin the batting to the wrong side of each silk piece for the bag, or use temporary spray adhesive to hold the layers together.

2. Refer to Figure 1 on page 130 for steps 2 and 4. With right sides together, stitch two 3 x 10 batting-backed strips and the 10-inch batting-backed squares together, leaving ¼ inch unstitched at the lower edge of each seam. Press the seams open. Repeat with the lining pieces.

3. Decide how many beaded tassels you want in each beaded cluster on the bag front, back and side panels. Choose an uneven number. Due to spacing variations, a specific width to cut the trim cannot be given. Cut a total of seven pieces of the required length for the clusters.

4. Fold the ribbon header so that the beaded fringe strands are closely clustered together—in halves, thirds or quarters, depending on your trim. Position the clusters on the bag panel with the top edge of the ribbon toward the bottom edge of the bag and the beads toward the top. Machine-stitch in place; use a zipper foot if necessary.

5. For the loops, turn under and press ¼ inch at each long edge of the 1½ x 19-inch strips. Fold in half with pressed edges even and stitch through all layers along both long edges (Figure 2 on page 130). Cut six 3-inch-long pieces from each strip.

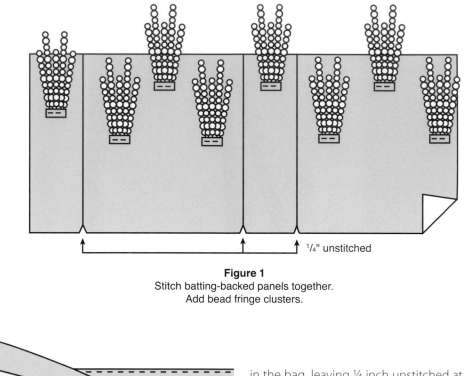

¼" unstitched

Figure 1
Stitch batting-backed panels together.
Add bead fringe clusters.

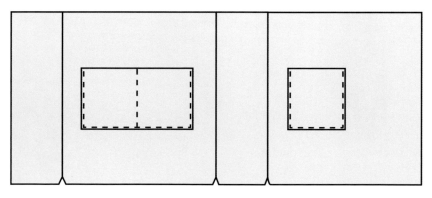

Figure 2
Fold strip and edgestitch.

6. Fold each short piece in half with raw edges even and pin to the upper edge of the bag, centering one strip on each side panel and spacing the remaining strips evenly. Remember to allow for ¼-inch-wide seam allowances at the two short edges when planning the spacing. Machine-baste the loops in place a scant ¼ inch from the raw edges. Sew the remaining side seam in the bag, leaving ¼ inch unstitched at the lower edge as you did for the previous seams.

7. To make the inside pockets for the lining, fold each rectangle in half crosswise and stitch the side and lower edges together, leaving an opening in the lower edge for turning. Clip the corners and turn right side out. Press, turning in the raw edges at the opening.

8. Pin the pockets in place on the lining front and back panels and edgestitch in place (Figure 3). Sew the remaining side seam in the lining, leaving ¼ inch unstitched at the bottom edge.

Figure 3
Sew pockets to lining.

9. Sew the bag bottom to the bottom edge of the bag. Begin by matching centers of the sides and bottom panels and stitch, ending at the seam lines. Then stitch the long edges together. The unstitched section of each seam will spread at the corners for smoothly turned corners. Turn the bag right side out. Repeat with the lining, leaving a 6-inch-long opening in one of the bottom seams for turning. *Do not turn the lining right side out.*

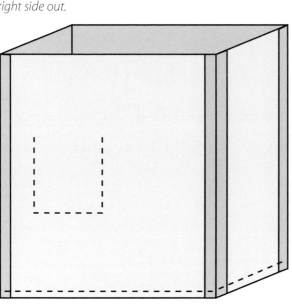

Figure 4
Assembled lining.

10. Slip the bag inside the lining with right sides facing and pin together with raw edges even. Machine-stitch ⅜ inch from the upper raw edges. Turn the bag right side out through the opening in the bottom of the lining. Turn in the lining opening edges and press. Edgestitch the layers together.

11. Tuck the lining into the bag, press the upper edge and edgestitch.

12. Flip the beads up and out of the way and hand-tack the ribbon header of each bead cluster in place again with several secure stitches, this time catching the lining in the stitches. If desired, use leftover beads to add individual bead accents to the bag (see bag photo).

13. Thread the cord through the loops. Butt the raw ends and secure with masking tape. Cut a 1½ x 2-inch piece of silk. Turn under and press the long edges, and then wrap the strip over the taped edges of the cord. Hand-sew in place. ●

A ROSE BY ANY OTHER NAME

DESIGN BY
LINDA TURNER GRIEPENTROG

A rose by any other name is still a rose and this one does double duty. Unpin the rolled-edge flower from this self-lined silk tote and use it as a pretty accent on a basic black evening dress, a wrap belt, hat or wrist bracelet.

FINISHED SIZE

9 x 7½ x 4 inches, excluding handles

MATERIALS

All yardages are for 44/45-inch-wide fabrics unless otherwise noted.

- 1 yard silk dupioni for bag and lining
- ½ yard 22-inch-wide stiff nonwoven interfacing
- ½ yard 24-inch-wide paper-backed fusible web
- 1 (¾-inch-diameter) magnetic snap for bag closure
- Pattern tracing paper or cloth
- 1½-inch-long jewelry pin back
- All-purpose thread to match fabric
- Rayon embroidery thread to match fabric
- Fabric/craft glue
- Rotary cutter, mat and ruler
- Basic sewing tools and equipment including serger

INSTRUCTIONS

Project Note: *All seam allowances are ½ inch wide unless otherwise noted.*

Cutting

- Enlarge the bag pattern (Figure 1) on pattern tracing paper and cut out.
- Use the bag pattern to cut four pieces from the silk dupioni, two pieces from the interfacing and two pieces from the fusible web.
- From the remaining silk, cut two 2½ x 17-inch strips for the handles and two 1½-inch squares for the closure reinforcement. For the rose, cut enough 2½-inch-wide true bias to make a strip 45 inches long. Piece as needed with bias seams and press the seams open.
- From the remaining interfacing, cut two 2¾ x 18-inch handle strips.
- On the fusible web, draw two 2-inch-diameter circles for the rose base. Cut out with a ¼-inch margin all around and apply to the wrong side of silk scraps. Cut out each circle and remove the backing paper. Following the manufacturer's directions, apply a silk circle to a scrap of stiff interfacing and cut out. Fuse the remaining silk circle to the other side of the interfacing.

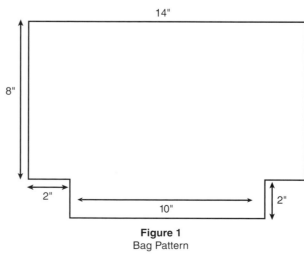

Figure 1
Bag Pattern

ASSEMBLY

1. Following the manufacturer's directions, apply the interfacing to the wrong side of two bag pieces. To reinforce the lining area where the snap closure will be placed, fuse the small silk square to the wrong side of the unbacked silk bag pieces as shown in Figure 2 below. Following the package directions, apply the magnetic closure to the reinforced areas of the bag lining.

2. With right sides together, sew the bag side and bottom seams; press the seams open. Sew the lining side seams and 1 inch of each bottom seam, leaving the center of the bottom seam open for turning (Figure 2). Backstitch at the beginning and end of each seam. Press the seams open.

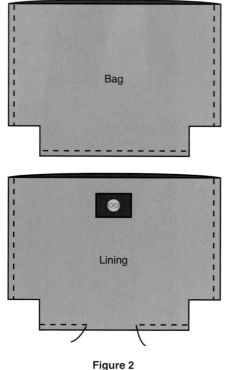

Figure 2
Sew bag and lining pieces together.

3. At each corner of the bag, align the side and bottom seam lines and stitch ½ inch from the raw edges. Stitch again ¼ inch from the first stitching and trim the seam close to the second row of stitching (Figure 3). Repeat with the lining. Turn the bag but not the lining right side out.

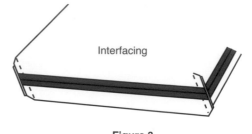

Figure 3
Align seams at each corner and stitch.

4. Fold each handle strip in half lengthwise with right sides together. Stitch ¼ inch from the long raw edges and press the seam open. Turn right side out and press, centering the seam on the underside. Insert a strip of stiff interfacing in each handle and trim excess even with handle end. Topstitch each handle ⅛ inch from each long edge.

5. Position a handle on the bag front and back as shown in Figure 4 and machine-baste ¼ inch from the raw edges.

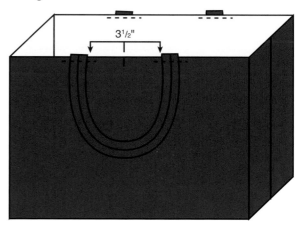

Figure 4
Sew handles to upper edge.

6. Slip the bag into the lining and pin with seams and raw edges aligned. Stitch ½ inch from the upper edge and trim the seam to ¼ inch. Carefully turn the bag right side out through the opening in the lining, being careful and taking your time to work the stiff bag fabric through the opening.

7. Turn under and press the opening edges in the lining. Stitch the turned edges together and tuck the completed lining inside the bag. Press the upper edge and topstitch ¼ inch from the pressed edge to hold the lining in place inside the finished bag.

8. Thread the serger with rayon embroidery thread in the upper and lower loopers and matching all-purpose thread in the needle. Adjust the serger for a narrow rolled edge. Serge one long edge of the bias strip, stretching the edge as you serge to ruffle it. Machine-baste ¼ inch from the remaining long edge.

9. Fold under one short end and then begin shaping the rose, drawing up the gathering stitches as needed. Hand-sew each round to the previous gathered edge as you go. To end, tuck the remaining short end underneath and tie off the basting thread to secure.

10. Glue the raw edges of the completed rose to the silk-covered circle and allow to dry.

11. Glue the pin back to the back of the rose and allow to dry. Pin in place on the bag front. ●

NOVEL
IDEAS

Make a statement with your bag. Use unusual fabrics,
interesting trims, and unusual materials to create
whimsical and interesting bags to carry for the fun of it.

ANYTHING BUT BLUE

DESIGN BY LUCY B. GRAY

Teens and jeans are a natural team-up. Celebrate this classic partnership by converting a pair of jazzy jeans into your next favorite handbag. The pockets are perfect for holding instant-access paraphernalia—think iPods and cell phones. Add some quick-to-make bag charms for added purse-onality.

INSTRUCTIONS

Project Note: *All seam allowances are ¼ inch wide unless otherwise noted.*

Cutting

• Zip the jeans zipper and snap the snap, then edgestitch the waistband edge to the underlayer to keep it permanently closed. Cut off the legs a few inches below the crotch seam. Set the legs aside for another recycling project.

• Undo the inseam stitching using a seam ripper.

• Open the crotch seam to the base of the zipper in front and to the level of the pocket bottoms in the back. Pick out all loose threads and press the crotch and upper-leg seam allowances as flat as possible.

FINISHED SIZE

15 x 9 x 5 inches

MATERIALS

• 1 pair brightly colored, recycled jeans (waist size 30 inches or smaller)
• ½ yard mid-weight printed fabric for the lining, color-coordinated with the jeans
• ½ yard contrasting cotton gingham for straps
• ½ yard polyester fleece
• All-purpose thread to match jeans and lining
• Flexible tape measure
• 9 x 12-inch piece plastic canvas
• Size 80/14 jeans sewing machine needle
• Size 8 leather hand-sewing needle
• Beeswax
• 2 to 3 small weights
• Spray-on fabric protector
• Temporary spray adhesive
• 16 x 20-inch sheet of gridded pattern tracing paper
• Quick-drying fabric glue
• Fine-tip permanent marking pen
• 2 sheets of paper towel
• Optional: Assorted charms (small stuffed animals, key ring charms)
• Rotary cutter, mat and ruler
• Basic sewing tools and equipment

- Stuff the jeans with a bed pillow and smooth the jeans over it. On both the front and back, arrange each separated crotch seam over the other so that they both lie completely flat.

Tuck pillow into cutoff jeans.

- Create a straight vertical seam below the fly in front by folding the top crotch/leg "flap" under itself and pinning it to the bottom crotch/leg flap. Use the ruler to align the new seam edge with the edge of the fly, making a perfectly straight line from waistband to bottom. In the same way, fold and pin the back crotch/upper leg seams to create a straight back seam.

Create straight seams at center back and center front.

- Edgestitch and topstitch the new seam to emulate the seam stitching in the jeans.

Note: *It's easiest to stitch from the bottom opening toward the waistline.*

- Arrange the jeans front side up so that they lie perfectly flat. Make sure the upper edges of the waistband are even and pin the layers together.
- Arrange the jeans on a rotary-cutting mat and place the ruler across the jeans at the point where the front leg seams meet. Cut along the upper edge of the ruler through both layers of the jeans.
- Turn the jeans wrong side out. Pin and stitch the cut edges together, creating the bag bottom. Turn the bag right side out again.
- Because each pair of jeans is different, you will need to make a custom-fitted bag lining. Use a flexible tape measure and record the following measurements:

A. Top of waistband to bottom seam at center front
B. Inside waistband circumference
C. Bottom seam

- Make a pattern for the lining by drawing a trapezoid on the sheet of gridded paper. Referring to Figure 1, begin the trapezoid by drawing a vertical line 1 inch longer than measurement A. For the top of the trapezoid, divide the waistband circumference (B) by 2 and add ¾ inch. For the base of the trapezoid, use the measurement of the bottom seam (C). Connect the two lines at each side.

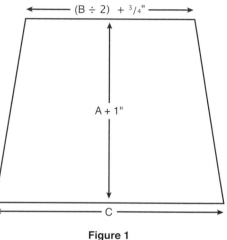

Figure 1
Make lining pattern.

- Connect the trapezoid's top and bottom lines.
- Cut out the paper pattern and use it to cut two lining pieces. Apply the temporary spray adhesive to the wrong side of each lining piece and smooth in place on the fleece. Cut out each fleece-backed piece. Turn the pieces over with the fleece side up and use the marking pen to draw lines on the fleece 1 inch from the upper edge and ¼ inch from the remaining edges. Gently lift the edges of the fleece so you can trim it away on the marked lines (Figure 2).

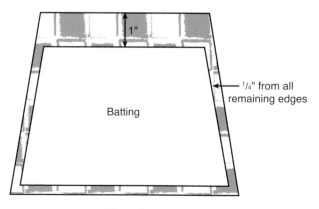

Figure 2
Trim batting along drawn lines.

- Machine-quilt the lining and batting layers together as desired.
- Enlarge the strap pattern (Figure 3) and cut four of each from the lining fabric and the gingham.

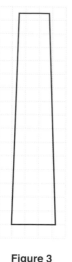

Figure 3
Strap Pattern
1 square = 1"

Assembly

1. Turn the jeans wrong side out. Fold each bottom corner with the side and bottom seam lines aligned. Draw a line 2½ inches from the point; pin the layers together. Stitch on the line, backstitching at each end. Stitch again ⅛ inch from the first stitching and trim off the point close to the second stitching (Figure 4).

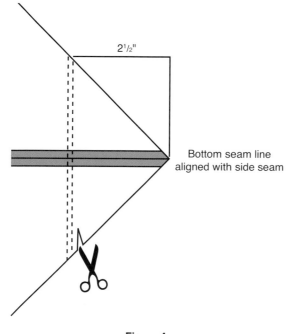

2½"

Bottom seam line
aligned with side seam

Figure 4
Stitch and trim.

2. Turn the bag right side out.

Bag with boxed bottom

3. Cut two pieces of plastic canvas to fit smoothly in the bottom of the bag. Place the canvas pieces together in the bag bottom. To keep them from shifting, run a thick bead of quick-drying fabric glue along the top piece of plastic canvas along the center seam in the bag. Use your fingers to smooth the mesh into the glue and onto the bottom seam allowance. Weight the plastic to hold it in contact with the seam allowance and allow the glue to dry.

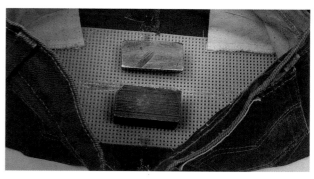

Glue plastic canvas in bag bottom and add weights.

4. If you want to add patch pockets or your own designer label to the lining, add them now.

5. With right sides facing, sew the two lining pieces together along the side and bottom edges, just catching the edges of the fleece in the stitching. Box the bottom corners as you did for the jeans bag, but draw the stitching line 2¼ inches from the point.

6. With right sides facing, sew each pair of straps together at the short end and press the seams open.

Apply spray adhesive to the wrong side of the gingham straps and smooth onto fleece. Cut out.

7. With right sides facing, sew the gingham/fleece strap to the lining strap. Turn right side out and press. Topstitch ⅛ inch from the long finished edges. **Optional:** *For added design punch, cut out a few designs from the lining fabric and glue or fuse them to the lower end of one of the straps.* Apply spray-on fabric protector to both sides of the completed strap.

8. Pin the straps to the jeans waistband so that a scant ¼ inch of each strap end lies below the lower edge of the waistband. Machine-stitch the straps at the waistband's top edge, following the stitching line of the waistband itself.

Note: *Don't try to sew through belt loops. Instead, undo the stitching and turn them out of the way. After machine-stitching the bag straps to the waistband, glue the belt loops back in place with quick-drying fabric glue.*

Hand-tack the base of the straps to the bottom of the waistband, using the size 8 leather needle to pierce the denim easily.

Stitch straps to inside of bag with ¼ inch extending past lower edge of waistband.

9. With wrong sides facing, place the bag lining inside the jeans bag. Turn under the upper edge of the lining so the edge is just below the upper edge of the waistband. Pin in place.

Note: *You may have to adjust the lining a bit by taking slightly deeper side seams to make it fit perfectly.*

10. Run several 15-inch-long pieces of sewing thread through the beeswax and press them between two sheets of paper towel to absorb excess wax. **Note:** *If you skip this step, the tough denim fabric of the jeans will shred the thread as you stitch.* Slipstitch the lining to the jeans waistband with tiny invisible stitches.

11. Press the lining edge if needed. ●

Add a Charm

Nothing "purse-onalizes" your jeans bag more than fun little bag charms dangling from the belt loops! Attach these customized charms to the belt loops with metal key clips or chains.

• Pick up small stuffed animals in dollar stores and re-outfit them to match the colors of your bag.

• Purchase short lengths of color-coordinated ribbon to make new neck bows for little dogs and bears.

• Glue a bright button to a band of ribbon to make a quirky dog tag. You can make several and change them often—the possibilities are endless!

M-M-M STRAWBERRIES!

DESIGN BY LUCY B. GRAY

Whip up this tasty little bucket tote using disposable containers from your kitchen. A built-in "bowl" in the lid holds a handful of realistic plastic strawberries. This delectable little bag is sure to turn heads and cause a few hunger pangs!

FINISHED SIZE

6 x 6 x 9 inches

MATERIALS

- 2 (⅝-yard) lengths medium-weight cotton fabric in coordinating prints or checks, one for outer fabric and one for lining
- ½ yard polyester fleece
- 2 (1 x 30-inch) strips nonwoven synthetic suede for the strap
- 1 (5 x 7-inch) piece of the same nonwoven synthetic suede
- 1 (1x 30-inch) strip of paper-backed fusible web
- 2 x 4-inch piece buckram or stiff nonwoven interfacing
- Pattern tracing paper or cloth
- 12 plastic strawberries
- 1¾-quart cardboard ice-cream carton
- 32-ounce plastic yogurt container
- 8-ounce plastic dairy-whip container
- Covered-button kit with 4 (⅞-inch-diameter) buttons
- 2 magnetic snap sets
- Optional: 6-inch-long zipper for lining
- All-purpose thread to match fabrics
- Carpet thread (or buttonhole twist) in neutral color
- Glover's needle
- Size 14/80 sewing machine needle
- ¼-inch-diameter leather punch
- Spray-on fabric protector
- Spray-on craft adhesive
- Quick-drying craft glue
- Rubber cement
- Transparent sticky tape
- 8 x 12-inch sheet sturdy cardboard
- 12 inches 24-gauge wire
- Small artist's brush
- Fine-tip permanent pen
- Sturdy craft scissors for cutting plastic containers
- Craft knife with #11 blade
- Basic sewing tools and equipment

INSTRUCTIONS

1. Collect and thoroughly wash the ice cream, yogurt and dairy-whip containers. Preshrink the cotton fabric for bag and press.

2. Refer to the photo. Trim away the cardboard "lip" at the upper edge of the ice-cream carton (A). Trim ⅛ inch from the edge of the ice-cream carton's lid (B). Cut the rim free from the plastic yogurt container (C) so ½ inch of plastic extends above the bottom. Cut down the plastic dairy-whip container (D) so it is ¾ inch high.

3. Using the artist's brush, paint the ice-cream carton's upper inside rim with quick-drying craft glue and put the brush in a cup of water until you have time to clean it thoroughly. Place the yogurt container rim inside the carton, align the top edges, and press the rim into the glue firmly. Place strips of sticky tape over the rim's edges to hold everything securely while the glue dries. For added stability, stitch the rim to the carton using carpet thread and a glover's needle.

4. To form the "bowl" for the fruit, glue the trimmed plastic dairy-whip container to the ice-cream carton lid. Allow several hours for the glue to harden.

5. From the outer fabric for the bag, cut one 8¼ x 16½-inch true-bias rectangle. From the lining fabric, cut one 6¼ x 14-inch true-bias rectangle. Apply craft adhesive to the lining wrong side and smooth onto a single layer of fleece, taking care not to stretch the fabric. Repeat with the outer fabric rectangle. Cut out each piece along the fabric cut edges.

6. With a permanent marker, draw lines on the fleece as shown in Figure 1. Trim away the fleece on the drawn lines and discard. (When trimmed, the fleece should measure 5 x 12½ inches on the lining and 5¼ x 15 inches on the outer fabric.) Machine-quilt both pieces and apply

spray-on fabric protector. Set the lining piece aside. Machine-baste ¼ inch from the upper long edge of the outer fabric/fleece rectangle. Turn under and press ¼ inch at one short edge.

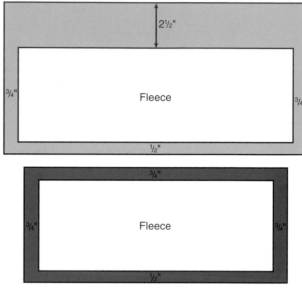

Figure 1
Trim fleece on outer fabric and lining pieces.

7. Apply an even coat of craft adhesive to the fleece side of the piece. Align the bottom edge of the carton with the lower edge of the fleece. Beginning at the unturned short edge, roll the carton evenly across the sticky fleece to adhere the fabric panel. The pressed short edge should cover the raw edge where they meet. Apply glue to the underside of the turned edge and glue it in place. Clip the fabric that extends beyond the bottom edge of the container to form small tabs.

8. Paint the bottom of the carton with craft glue around the perimeter, making the glue circle ½ inch wide. Turn the fabric tabs to the underside of the carton and smooth into the glue.

9. Measure the diameter of the carton bottom and cut a synthetic suede circle to fit. Glue to the bottom of the carton to cover the fabric raw edges.

10. With craft glue, paint a ½-inch-wide strip along the upper edge on the inside of the plastic yogurt lip in the carton. Draw up the basting at the upper edge of the fabric on the carton so it pulls to the inside. Use your fingers to smooth the fabric in place in the glue, distributing the gathers evenly. Set the carton aside for a few hours until the glue has dried completely.

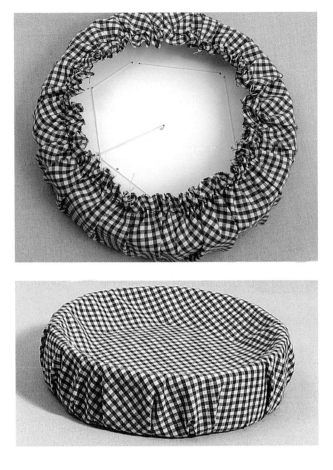

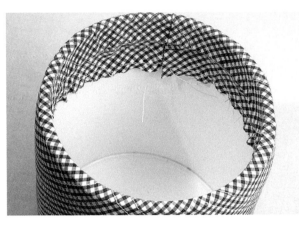

11. Glue strips of fleece to the sides of the lid to pad the junction of the yogurt container with the ice-cream lid. Cut a 10-inch-diameter circle of outer fabric. Machine-baste ½ inch from the outer edge, leaving thread tails. Apply fabric protector. Place the lid, "bowl" side down, in the center of the circle.

13. Trace the templates on page 147 onto pattern tracing paper and cut out. Use snap flap pattern to cut four snap flaps from the synthetic suede. Cut two from the buckram or heavy nonwoven interfacing and trim ¼ inch away all around. Remove the wire shank from two of the covered-button tops so that after being covered, the buttons can be glued in place. Cover the two buttons with outer-fabric scraps following the kit directions. Install the ball half of the magnetic snap on two of the suede flaps. Glue the buckram pieces over the wrong side of the snaps. Trim ¼ inch from the straight edge of the two remaining suede flaps and glue a covered button to the right side of each flap. With wrong sides together and curved edges aligned, glue the button flaps to the magnetic-snap flaps and set aside.

12. Draw up the basting to gather the fabric up and over the sides of the lid. Adjust for a snug fit and tie off the threads. Using neutral carpet thread and a glover's needle, tack the fabric to the bowl. When you flip the lid over there will be a "bowl" in the top of the lid.

14. Cut a 5-inch-diameter circle from sturdy cardboard. Trim the circle as needed so it fits easily inside the lid. Spray the cardboard circle with craft adhesive and cover it with fleece; trim the excess fleece even with the circle edge.

15. Cut a circle of lining fabric 1½ inches larger in diameter than the fleece-covered circle. Apply fabric protector. Apply craft adhesive to one side of the fleece and center it on the wrong side of the lining circle. Clip the outer edge of the fabric circle and turn the raw edges to the underside of the cardboard. Glue in place. Glue the completed lining circle into the lid. Using rubber cement, glue the button flaps to the inside of the lid opposite each other. Use a few hand stitches to anchor the flaps to the fabric in the lid for added durability.

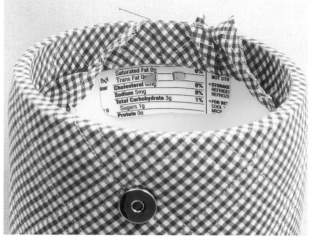

Note From the Designer: *I used fabric recycled from designer shirts for the lining and outer fabric, and salvaged their labels and stitched them to the lining circle before assembling it and gluing it in the lid. I also added my own label. Fun!*

16. Place the lid on the carton and mark the positioning for the socket halves of the magnetic snaps. Use the perforated disk from the snap set to mark the position for the vertical slits. Cut the slits with a craft knife, and insert the female snap halves. Cut two 1 x 2-inch pieces of plastic from the dairy-whip container; make corresponding slits for the snap prongs and position inside under the fabric edge. Apply the snaps.

17. To make the bag strap, fuse the two suede strips together with the strip of fusible web. Use a press cloth to protect the suede. Trim the ends using the strap end pattern piece and punch a hole in each end with the leather punch. Using the size 14 sewing machine needle, edgestitch around the strap. Use an edgestitching foot to help keep the stitching equidistant from the edges.

18. Place the lid on the carton and fasten the magnetic snap halves together. Mark with pins where the straps go, placing them opposite each other between the snap flaps. Cover the other two buttons with outer-fabric scraps, following kit directions. To anchor each strap end, punch two holes in the carton with the glover's needle. Thread a 6-inch length of 24-gauge wire through one carton hole from the inside to the outside, then through the strap hole, the shank of the button and back through the strap hole and into the carton.

19. Cut two 1 x 2-inch pieces of container plastic and poke two holes in each of the centers. Thread the wire ends through the holes in the plastic pieces and twist them tightly together. Press the wire flat and cover with sticky tape. Paint all four plastic pieces with craft glue and press the gathered outer fabric into it.

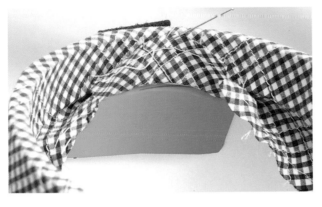

20. Turn under and press ¼ inch along the upper edge and one short edge of the quilted lining panel. Make shallow snips along the bottom edge so the lining will curve smoothly around the carton's inside lower edge. Spray the fleece side with craft adhesive and place the lining right side out inside the carton. Smooth the lining in place and glue the short turned edge in place over the short raw edge inside the carton. Glue the turned upper edge of the lining in place.

21. Cut a 5-inch cardboard circle and trim it to fit easily into the bottom of the carton. Cover the circle with fleece

and then the lining fabric as you did for the inside of the lid. Paint the inside bottom of the carton with craft glue and press the bottom circle firmly into the glue.

22. Glue the strawberries in the bowl on the lid and allow a full day for the glue to harden. ●

Recycle It!

Food is sold in cardboard containers that are lightweight but engineered to withstand great stress, and that makes them terrific for handbag infrastructures. Cylinders of different sizes, half-gallon tubs, and rectangular boxes all have great design possibilities. Use the methods shown in this chapter to reinforce the containers and create lids that fit snugly.

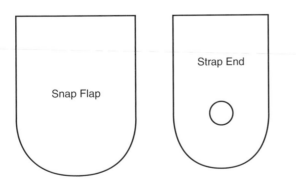

Snap Flap

Strap End

Templates for M-M-M Strawberries!
Actual Size

BEAUTY IN THE BAG

DESIGN BY LYNN WEGLARZ

Fake fur and colorful satin make a fashion statement in this great little bag. Use it to pack your beauty essentials when traveling, and then use it as a fun evening bag, too. Tucked inside is a matching sleep mask for a beautiful night's rest—or a stylish sleep statement while napping en route.

INSTRUCTIONS

Project Note: *Use ¼-inch-wide seam allowances. Read Sewing on Fake Fur on page 151 before you begin.*

FINISHED SIZES

Bag: 11 x 10 x 3 inches
Sleep Mask: 4½ x 9 inches

MATERIALS

Yardages are based on 58/60-inch-wide fabrics.

- ⅜ yard fake fur
- ⅜ yard satin for lining
- ⅜ yard thin cotton batting
- Pattern tracing paper or cloth
- Marking pen
- ½-inch-diameter magnetic snap set
- ⅜ yard ¼-inch-wide elastic
- Scrap of fusible interfacing
- All-purpose threads to match fabrics
- Optional: temporary spray adhesive
- Basic sewing tools and equipment

Cutting

- Enlarge the bag and mask pattern pieces (Figure 1) on pattern tracing cloth and cut out.

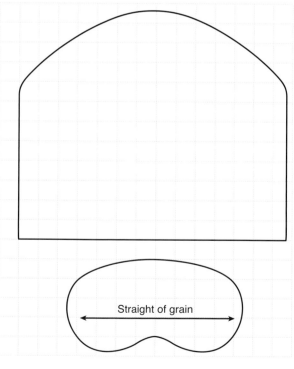

Straight of grain

Figure 1
Patterns for Bag and Eye Mask.
1 square = 1"

• Use the bag pattern to cut two pieces each from the fake fur, lining fabric and batting.

• Use the mask pattern to cut one each from fake fur and lining fabric.

• From the remaining lining fabric, cut one 6 x 14-inch strip for the bag handle. For the mask, cut enough 1½-inch-wide bias strips to make a strip 26 inches long, piecing strips together if necessary.

Assembly

1. With right sides together, sew the two fur bag pieces together along the side and bottom edges.

2. Position a piece of batting on the wrong side of each bag lining piece and baste in place a scant ¼ inch from the raw edges (or use temporary spray adhesive to secure the layers).

3. With right sides facing, sew the lining pieces together along the side and bottom edges, leaving a 6-inch-long opening for turning (Figure 2). Do not turn the lining right side out.

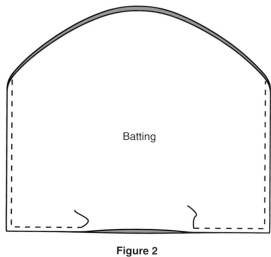

Figure 2
Sew bag pieces together. Sew lining pieces together, leaving a 6" opening in lining.

4. Box the bottom of the bag by folding each corner with side and bottom seams aligned; pin. Stitch 1½ inches from the point and again ¼ inch from the first stitching (Figure 3). Trim close to the second row of stitches and turn right side out. Repeat with the lining, but do not turn right side out.

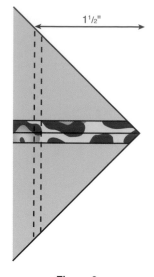

Figure 3
Align side and bottom seam lines.
Stitch 1½" from point.

5. Apply a 1½-inch square of fusible interfacing to the wrong side of the lining front and back at the snap location to reinforce the fabric. Apply the snap parts to the lining following the package directions (Figure 4).

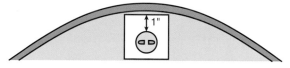

Figure 4
Stabilize area under snap locations
before applying snaps to lining.

6. Fold the satin strip in half lengthwise with right sides facing and stitch ¼ inch from the long raw edges. Press the seam to one side. Turn right side out and press, centering the seam line on the underside. Fold the satin strap in half with the seam inside and raw edges even. Center the folded strap on the right side at the upper edge of the bag back with raw edges even. Machine-baste a scant ¼ inch from the raw edges.

7. Tuck the fur bag into the lining with seam lines matching and raw edges even; stitch. Turn the bag right side out through the opening in the lining. Turn under and press the opening edges and stitch together.

8. With wrong sides together, baste the fur mask to the lining mask. Position the elastic on the lining and pin in place. Test the fit around your head and adjust the elastic length as needed. Machine-baste in place.

9. Use the bias strip of lining fabric to bind the outer edges of the mask. Stitch it to the fake fur side, wrap to the underside, turn under the raw edge and slipstitch in place. ●

Sewing on Fake Fur

Read through these sewing tips before you begin.

• Use a "with nap" cutting layout so when you run your hand from the top to the bottom the fur is smooth (not rough as when you pet a cat in the "wrong" direction).

• Pin pattern pieces to the backing side of the fur.

• Cut pieces single layer using only the tips of your dressmaker's shears. Some sewers prefer using a mat knife or a single-edge razor blade.

• Cut the backing only to avoid a lot of fur fuzz on your cutting table.

• Use a new 90/14 universal needle.

• Push the fur pile away from the raw edge of the seam, to the inside of the seam. Using a damp sponge to do this helps.

• Adjust the stitch for a 4mm-wide, 2mm-long zigzag stitch and sew so that the left swing of the needle stitches at the seam line and the right swing goes over the raw edges.

• Open the seam and brush along the seam line, or use a pin to lift the fur out of the stitches.

FIESTA FANCY

DESIGN BY NANCY FIEDLER

Flirty organza ruffles that you make on your serger jazz up a festive print in this little drawstring bag. Purchased trims and ribbons are other options for your own version of this tote that's sure to bring a smile to anyone's face. There's a divided pocket inside to keep things organized and safe in this sassy little tote.

INSTRUCTIONS

Project Note: *Use ¼-inch-wide seams unless otherwise noted.*

Cutting

• From the print fabric, cut two strips 12½ x 22½ inches, one 10½ x 22½-inch strip for the pocket and two 7-inch-diameter circles for the bottom.

FINISHED SIZE

7 x 12 inches

MATERIALS

All yardages are for 44/45-inch-wide fabrics.

• 1⅛ yards printed cotton for bag and lining (black multicolor print)
• ¾ yard polyester organza (black)
• ⅜ yard medium-weight fusible interfacing
• ¼ yard heavyweight sew-in interfacing
• 2 yards each of 2 different colors of rattail cord (black and red)

• Barrel beads in assorted coordinating colors
• 1 cone texturized nylon thread in colors to coordinate with the fabric print
• All-purpose thread to match fabrics
• Chalk marker
• Rotary cutter, mat and ruler
• New size 11 sewing machine and serger needles
• Bodkin or large pin for threading the drawstrings through the casing
• Liquid seam sealant
• Basic sewing tools and equipment

• Cut one 7-inch-diameter circle from the heavyweight sew-in interfacing.
• Cut six 3 x 45-inch strips of organza for the ruffles.

Assembly

1. To make the inside pocket, fold the 10½ x 22½-inch strip in half lengthwise with wrong sides together and press. Align the long raw edges with one long edge of the lining and machine-baste a scant ¼ inch from the raw edges. Mark and stitch on the dividing lines as shown in Figure 1.

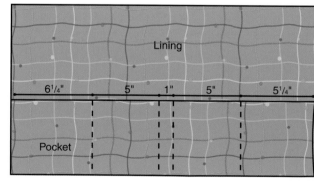

Figure 1
Stitch pocket panel to lining.

2. Fold the lining in half with right sides facing so it measures 11¼ x 12½-inches. Stitch ¼ inch from the long raw edges. Press the seam open. With right sides together, stitch a fabric circle to one edge of the lining tube (Figure 2). Set the lining aside.

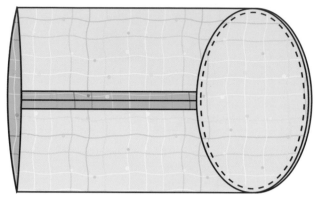

Figure 2
Stitch lining tube to circle.

3. Following the manufacturer's directions, apply fusible interfacing to the wrong side of the remaining fabric rectangle.

4. With chalk or other removable marker that will show on the fabric right side, mark ruffle placement lines on the rectangle (Figure 3). Also mark buttonholes as shown.

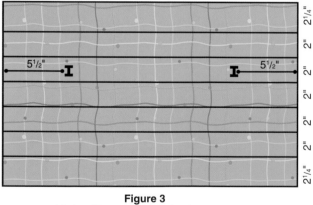

Figure 3
Mark ruffle and buttonhole placement.

5. Make a ½-inch-long buttonhole at each buttonhole marking on the bag body (not on the lining) and cut the buttonholes open.

6. Adjust the serger for a rolled edge (see A Perfect Rolled Edge on page 155). Roll-edge–finish both long edges of each organza ruffle strip, trimming away ¼ inch with the serger knife as you go so the finished strips are about 1½ inches wide.

7. Adjust the sewing machine for a slightly longer than normal stitch length (3.5–4mm). Machine-stitch through the center of each strip. Do not lock the stitching at the beginning, but do lock it at the end of the strip by backstitching or stitching in place.

8. Pull up the bobbin thread to gather each organza strip so it measures 22½ inches long. Tie off the threads securely and adjust the gathers evenly. Center a strip on one of the marked lines on the bag and stitch in place on top of the row of gathering.

9. With right sides facing and ruffle ends matching, stitch the raw edges of the bag together as for the lining. Press the seam open.

10. Baste the interfacing circle to the wrong side of the remaining fabric circle. Sew the interfaced circle to the lower edge of the bag tube as for the lining. Take care not to catch the lower edge of the bottom ruffle in the stitching.

11. Slip the ruffled bag into the lining with right sides together. Stitch around the upper edge, leaving a 6-inch-long opening for turning. Turn the bag right side out. Turn under and press the opening edges along the seam lines. Slipstitch the edges together. Topstitch ⅛ inch from the upper edge of the bag.

12. To create the drawstring casing, stitch around the bag through all layers at each end of the buttonholes. Take care to keep the ruffles free from the stitching.

13. Thread one piece of rattail cord through the buttonholes, with both ends exiting the casing at one side of the bag. Repeat with the second cord. Slip the cord ends through one or more beads and tie the ends together with overhand knots to secure. Treat the cord ends with liquid seam sealant to prevent fraying. ●

A Perfect Rolled Edge

Texturized nylon thread (woolly nylon) is made of unspun nylon fibers. When doing rolled-edge serging, using this type of thread in the loopers of the serger gives better coverage and a better rolled edge than you can achieve when using all-purpose serger thread.

To serge a rolled-edge hem:

1. Adjust the serger for a 3-thread rolled edge as directed in your owner's manual.

2. Thread both loopers with the nylon thread and use regular serger thread in the needle.

3. Shorten the stitch length to 1.5mm or the rolled-hem setting on your serger.

4. Tighten the tension of the lower looper 3–4 numbers higher than the normal setting. Place a test strip of the fabric to be hemmed right side up under the presser foot. Serge along the edge of the fabric just skimming it with the serger knife. This will allow any uneven edges to be smoothed out by the cutting action of the knife.

5. Check the strip to see that the hem has rolled to the back. If not, tighten the lower looper tension and test again. Sometimes the upper looper tension may need to be loosened slightly to achieve the perfect rolled edge. Keep testing until you have created the desired look.

JEWELS IN THE ROUND

DESIGN BY PAULINE RICHARDS

Whether you're off to the gym or packing for a trip to the far reaches of the globe, your jewelry will be safe in a soft, padded round bag. Specialty decorative zippers sit atop the finished rounds to show off their woven tapes that are too pretty to hide.

FINISHED SIZE
7 inches diameter

MATERIALS
Note: *Materials are given for one bag.*
- ⅓ yard fabric for outside
- ⅓ yard lining fabric
- ¼ yard fleece
- Temporary spray adhesive
- All-purpose thread to match lining fabric
- All-purpose thread to match zipper tape
- 4 inches of 2 narrow ribbons for the zipper pull
- 7-inch zipper with decorative zipper tape (Riri; see Sewing Sources on page 175.)
- 7-inch-diameter circle of heavy paper
- Air- or water-soluble marking pen
- Wonder Tape
- Rotary cutter, mat and ruler
- Basic sewing tools and equipment

INSTRUCTIONS
Cutting
- Cut two 9-inch fabric squares each from the outside and lining fabrics, and fleece.
- From the lining fabric, cut a 1¼ x 22-inch piece of true bias for the outer-edge binding.

Assembly
1. Apply a light coat of temporary spray adhesive to one side of each piece of fleece and smooth in place on the wrong side of the outside fabric squares. Apply a light coat of adhesive to the remaining side of each fleece square and smooth a lining piece in place on top, face up.

2. Cut one layered square in half and bind the raw edges (Figure 1).

Figure 1
Bind long cut edges of layered piece.

3. Apply Wonder Tape to the wrong side of the zipper tape at both long edges. Remove the protective paper and position the zipper on the right side of one rectangle with the zipper teeth ¼ inch from the finished edge (Figure 2 on page 158).

Note: *Illustration shows how it looks from the lining side.*

Wonder Tape

Figure 2
Position bound edge on wrong side of zipper.

4. Thread the machine with thread to match the zipper tape and stitch close to the outer long edges of the zipper tape. Repeat step 3 and 4 with the remaining rectangle and the other half of the zipper (Figure 3).

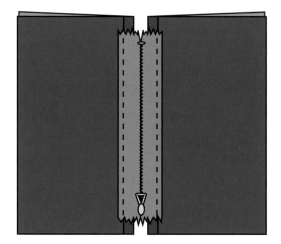

Figure 3
Sew zipper to outside of layered rectangles.

5. Adjust your machine for a wide satin stitch and stitch over the zipper tapes just beyond the zipper top and bottom stops (Figure 4).

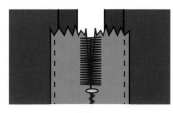

Figure 4
Satin-stitch zipper tapes together at each end of zipper.

6. *Optional:* *If desired, machine-quilt the layers together beyond the zipper tape as shown in the silver round. Lines are spaced ½ inch apart and end ¼ inch from the zipper edges. See Graph-It on page 159.*

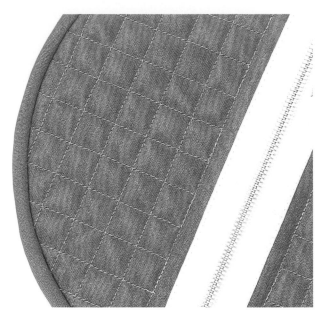

7. Fold the paper circle in half and crease. Open the circle and place on top of the zippered square with the crease along the center of the zipper teeth. Make sure the length of the zipper is centered in the circle. Mark the outer edge of the circle on the square using a marking pen. Place the remaining layered square under the marked zipper square with the linings facing each other; pin the layers together. Adjust the machine for 10 stitches per inch and stitch on the marked line. Cut out the circle ⅛ inch from the stitching (Figure 5).

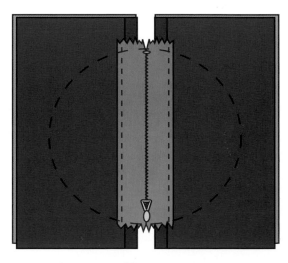

Figure 5
Stitch zippered square to backing square along circle.

8. With right sides facing and using a ¼-inch-wide seam allowance, sew the binding to the outer edge of the circle. Turn the bias to the back over the raw edges, turn under the raw edge along the stitching; slipstitch in place.

9. Fold the ribbons in half, insert the folded end through the hole in the zipper pull and then pull the ribbon threads through the loop and tighten. ●

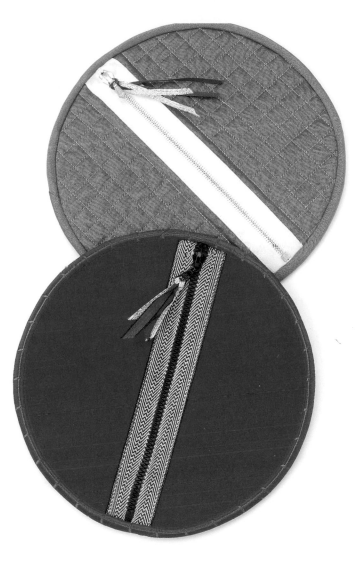

Graph-It!

For perfectly aligned rows of quilting, use graph-paper stitching guides.

1. Cut two 5 x 8½-inch strips of graph paper (4 squares per inch) position along the zipper edges and pin in place. Make sure the graph lines are perfectly aligned.

2. Thread your machine with decorative or matching thread and stitch along the first graph line on each side of the zipper.

3. Skip one line and stitch on the next. Continue in this fashion to quilt all the vertical lines on each half of the zipper square.

4. Stitch horizontal rows on each half.

5. Carefully tear away the graph paper.

PRETTY AS A POSY

DESIGN BY PAM LINDQUIST

Your favorite little girl will love this posy purse complete with a bumblebee button closure.

INSTRUCTIONS

Project Note: All seam allowances are ½ inch wide.

Cutting

- Enlarge the pattern for the outer flower Stitching Guide as directed on page 164. Draw on pattern tracing or tissue paper and cut out. Set aside for the flower assembly.
- Enlarge the pattern shapes for the center and inner flower shapes and the flower center as directed on page 164 onto template plastic and cut out.

FINISHED SIZE

6½ x 9 inches, excluding straps

MATERIALS

- 2 (9 x 13-inch) rectangles for the purse body
- ½ yard green polka-dot print for binding and strap
- 8-inch square medium pink tone-on-tone print
- 2 (10-inch) squares dark pink tone-on-tone print
- 6-inch square dark pink tone-on-tone print
- 5-inch square yellow tone-on-tone print
- 10-inch square muslin or other cotton scrap
- 2 (6½ x 9-inch) rectangles thin cotton batting
- 10-inch square batting
- All-purpose thread to match fabrics
- ½ yard paper-backed fusible web
- 2 yards fine decorative cord or yarn for flower center or substitute small beads, buttons or hot-fix crystals
- Bee button for purse closure
- 10-inch-long piece ¼-inch-wide green ribbon for closure
- Template plastic
- Pattern tracing or tissue paper
- Pencil
- Air- or water-soluble marking pen
- Zipper foot
- Rotary cutter, mat and ruler
- Basic sewing tools and equipment

- Trace around the two flower shapes and the flower center on the paper side of the fusible web. Cut out, leaving a ¼-inch margin all around each shape.
- Position the shapes on the wrong side of the correct fabric as noted on each pattern and fuse in place following the manufacturer's directions. Cut out the shapes on the drawn lines.
- From the green polka-dot fabric, cut enough 3-inch-wide bias strips to make a 50-inch-long strip for the binding and strap. Sew the strips together with bias seams and press the seams open.

Assembly

1. Apply a 10-inch square of fusible web to the wrong side of the remaining dark pink square of fabric. Remove the backing paper and fuse the square to the 10-inch muslin square.

2. Remove the backing paper from the medium pink flower and *center it* on the right side of the dark pink square. Fuse in place. Satin-stitch over the raw edges. Remove the backing paper on the dark pink flower. Center it on the medium pink flower and fuse in place. Satin-stitch over the raw edges. Repeat with the yellow flower center (Figure 1 on page 162).

3. With the right side up, place the completed flower square on top of the 10-inch square of batting. Place the muslin-backed dark pink square face down on top of the flower. Pin the layers together. Center the paper stitching guide on top of the squares and stitch around the outer edge of the pattern (Figure 2 on page 162).

Figure 1
Center shapes on dark pink muslin-backed square.
Fuse in place and satin-stitch over edges.

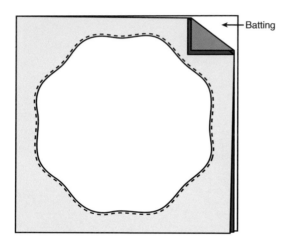

← Batting

Figure 2
Pin stitching guide to layered squares.
Stitch around outer edge.

4. Remove the pattern and pins, and trim the excess fabric ¼ inch from the stitching. Slash the underlayer as shown in Figure 3 and turn the flower right side out through the opening. Press.

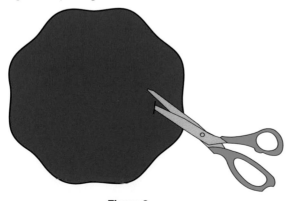

Figure 3
Slash backing layer only.
Make slash a few inches from the outer edge.

5. Satin-stitch over the finished outer edge of the flower. Attach decorative cord to the flower center by hand or couch it in place by machine. Alternatively, decorate the flower center with beads, buttons or hot-fix crystals.

6. Position each 6½ x 9-inch rectangle of batting on the wrong side at one end of a 9 x 13-inch green rectangle and baste in place.

7. Fold each rectangle in half along the long edge of the batting with right sides out. Quilt each piece as desired and round off the lower corners using the edge of a small plate or glass as your guide. Machine-baste ¼ inch from the raw edges. Center the flower over the purse back as shown in Figure 4, making sure the slash in the back of the flower is completely hidden against the back. Machine-stitch just inside the satin stitching to secure the flower to the purse back.

Front

Quilt layers with batting in between.

Back

Stitch just inside satin stitching.

Figure 4
Quilt the front and back panels
and add the appliqué flower.

8. On the inside, slipstitch the upper edge of the purse to the back of the flower. Position the remaining purse piece on top of the purse back and machine-baste ¼ inch from the raw edges (Figure 5).

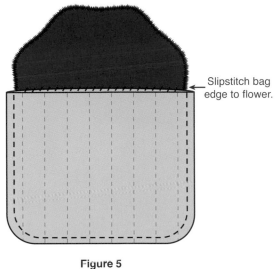

→ Slipstitch bag edge to flower.

Figure 5
Baste front and back pieces together.

9. Sew the short ends of the 3 x 50-inch polka-dot strip together to make a circle. Fold the strip in half with wrong sides together and raw edges even; press.

10. Beginning at the upper edge on one side of the purse, align the raw edges of the binding strip with the purse raw edges and pin in place. Stitch ½ inch from the raw edges, beginning and ending the stitching at the upper edge of the purse. Turn the binding over the raw edges to the other side of the purse and slipstitch in place. Turn under and press the remainder of the binding to make the strap; slipstitch the turned edges together.

11. Fold the 10-inch-long piece of ribbon in half to make a loop and fit around the button. Tack the ribbon together to make the loop, and then tack the loop to the underside of the posy flap. Tie the ends of the ribbon in a bow and tack it in place. Sew the button in place on the purse front. ●

Sunflowers Please

Use the alternate flower petal to create a sunflower flap for an autumn version of the posy purse.

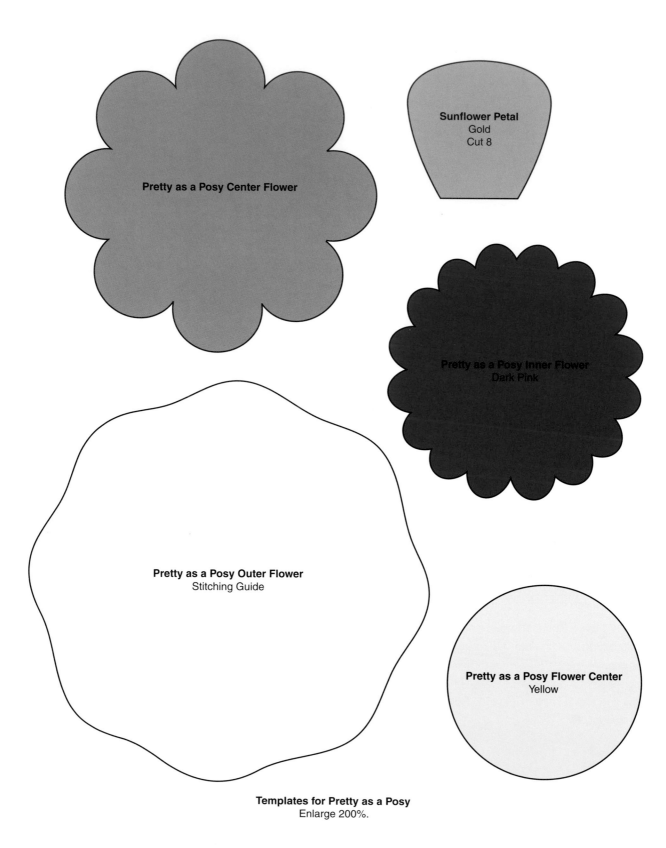

Sunflower Petal
Gold
Cut 8

Pretty as a Posy Center Flower

Pretty as a Posy Inner Flower
Dark Pink

Pretty as a Posy Outer Flower
Stitching Guide

Pretty as a Posy Flower Center
Yellow

Templates for Pretty as a Posy
Enlarge 200%.

ROLL IT UP

DESIGN BY JULIE WEAVER

Carry your make-up in this handy little clutch. It sews up in a snap and easily fits into a tote or suitcase. You'll want to make several for yourself and for gifts.

INSTRUCTIONS

Cutting

- Cut a 12 x 22-inch rectangle from the stripe, yellow and clear vinyl fabrics and from the batting.
- Cut a 9-inch square of vinyl for the inside pocket panel.
- From the yellow solid, cut two 3 x 9-inch strips for the pocket binding and two 3 x 44-inch strips for the outer edge binding.
- Sandwich the 12 x 22-inch piece of batting between the wrong sides of the striped and solid fabrics. Place the vinyl on top of the solid fabric.
- On a 12 x 22-inch piece of tissue paper or pattern tracing paper, draw a 1-inch diagonal grid. Place on top of the vinyl. Stitch on the grid lines to quilt all layers together (Figure 1). Tear away the tissue.
- Enlarge the pattern (Figure 2) on pattern tracing paper or tissue paper. Cut it out and pin it in place on the quilted layers. Cut out.

Assembly

1. Center the loop half of the hook-and-loop tape on the vinyl side of the quilted panel 1 inch from the upper curved edge. Stitch in place. Flip the lower edge of the vinyl pocket out of the way and pin the hook half of the tape to the striped side of the

FINISHED SIZE

6 x 9 inches closed;
9 x 17 inches open

MATERIALS

All yardages based on 44/45-inch-wide fabric.

- ⅓ yard striped pique or other similar-weight woven cotton fabric
- ½ yard coordinating yellow solid fabric for lining and binding
- Pink, yellow and green fabric scraps for flower
- ⅓ yard clear vinyl fabric
- ⅓ yard thin cotton batting
- 3-inch-long strip hook-and-loop tape
- Pattern tracing paper or tissue paper
- All-purpose thread to match fabrics
- Size 80/14 universal needle
- Basic sewing supplies and tools

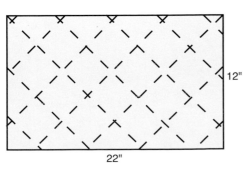

12"

22"

Figure 1
Quilt the layers together.

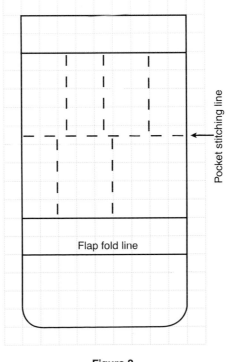

Pocket stitching line

Flap fold line

Figure 2
Roll It Up Pattern
1 square = 1"

quilted panel with the upper edge 2½ inches from the straight edge. Stitch in place (Figure 3).

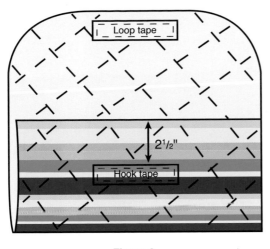

Figure 3
Sew hook tape to fabric panel.

2. Fold the vinyl square in half with short edges even and crease. Unfold.

3. Fold the 9-inch-long binding strips in half lengthwise with wrong sides together and press. Sew one piece of binding to each of two opposite edges of the 9-inch vinyl square. Fold the binding over the raw edges to the right side of the vinyl and edgestitch (Figure 4).

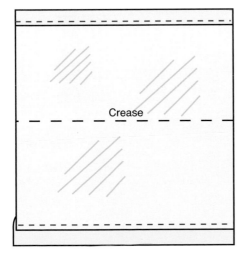

Figure 4
Bind opposite edges of vinyl square.

4. Position one bound edge of the vinyl 2 inches above the lower straight edge of the quilted fabric panel. Stitch in place along the center crease (Figure 5).

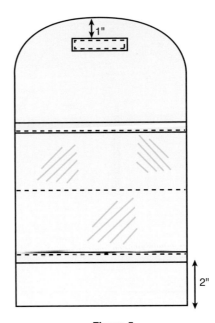

Figure 5
Stitch bound vinyl panel to fabric panel along center crease.

5. Cut a 9-inch square of tissue paper and draw the pocket stitching lines on it (see Figure 2). Position it on top of the bound vinyl pocket and machine-stitch on each line. Backstitch at the beginning and end of each row of stitching.

Note: *You can customize the pocket sizes for the items you wish to store in the roll-up.*

6. Sew the two long binding strips together with bias seams and press the seams open. Fold the strip in half with wrong sides together and press.

7. Pin and sew the binding to the vinyl side of the quilted panel, mitering the corners as you reach them. Wrap the binding to the right side over the raw edges and edgestitch in place through all layers.

8. Trace the flower and two leaves (see page 169) on the wrong side of the pink and green fabrics. Layer each piece of fabric with a matching piece on top of a scrap of batting. Stitch just inside the lines and cut out each piece leaving a scant ¼-inch-wide seam allowance all around. Clip seams at inner points on the flowers and across the points on the leaves. Make a small slit in the top layer of fabric in each piece (Figure 6 on page 168). Turn each piece right side out through the slit; press. Whipstitch the slit edges to the batting.

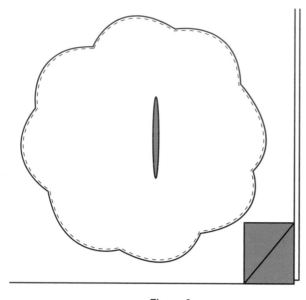

Figure 6
Stitch just inside drawn lines.
Make slit in top fabric layer.
Cut out ⅛" from stitching.

10. Arrange the flower, flower center and leaves on the clutch flap and sew in place, catching only the fabric and batting layers in the stitching. ●

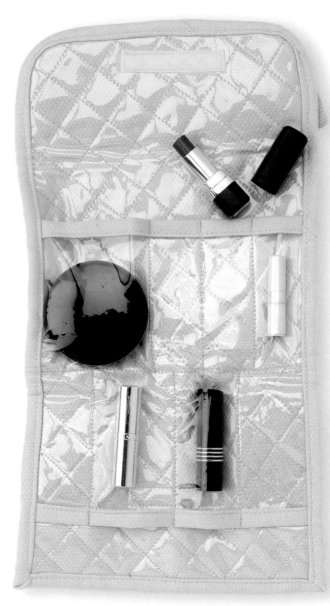

9. For the flower center, cut one 3¼-inch-diameter circle from the yellow solid fabric. Turn under ⅛ inch along the outer edge and hand-baste in place. Leave the needle threaded and draw up the basting to gather the circle and flatten it in the center (Figure 7). Draw the needle and thread to the underside and take several stitches in place to secure the gathers.

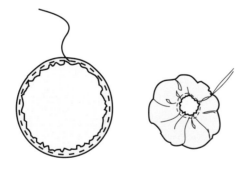

Figure 7
Make yo-yo flower center.

Templates for Roll It Up
Actual Size

ZIPPER-DEE-DO-DA

DESIGN BY STEPHANIE CORINA GODDARD

Pair a whimsical cotton print with multihued plastic zippers to make this handy little clutch. Use it for sorting scarves, hosiery or jewelry when you pack for your travels or as a drop-in organizer to make changing purses a breeze. Use a dressy fabric such as velvet or satin and rhinestone-studded versions for a pretty clutch.

INSTRUCTIONS

Project Note: *Unless otherwise indicated, use ½-inch-wide seam allowances.*

FINISHED SIZE
8 x 10 inches

MATERIALS
- ⅜ yard 44/45-inch-wide print for bag
- ⅜ yard 44/45-inch-wide lining
- 19 x 23-inch rectangle polyester fleece
- 3 plastic sport zippers (Riri), 12 inches or longer in coordinating colors. See Options for Two-Tone Zips on page 174 and Sewing Sources on page 175.
- All-purpose thread to match fabric
- Pattern tracing paper
- Air-soluble fabric-marking pen
- Optional: temporary spray adhesive
- Size 14/90 sewing machine needle
- Zipper foot
- Needle-nose pliers
- Optional: walking foot
- Basic sewing tools and equipment

Note: *Substitute zippers with rhinestone-studded teeth for a dressy clutch made from velvet, silk dupioni or a pretty brocade.*

Cutting
- From the print for the bag, cut two 9 x 11-inch rectangles for the bag front and back, one 5½ x 11-inch lower pocket rectangle and one 7¼ x 11-inch upper pocket rectangle.
- Repeat with the lining and the batting.

Assembly
1. Using the air-soluble marking pen and working from the bottom up, draw horizontal lines on the right side of each pocket, spacing them 1½ inches apart (Figure 1 on page 172). Repeat with the front and back rectangles.

2. Arrange the large marked rectangles for the bag front and back face up on a corresponding piece of batting. Insert the size 14/90 needle in the sewing machine and select a decorative stitch. Attach a walking foot if available. Stitch through all layers on the marked lines on each piece.

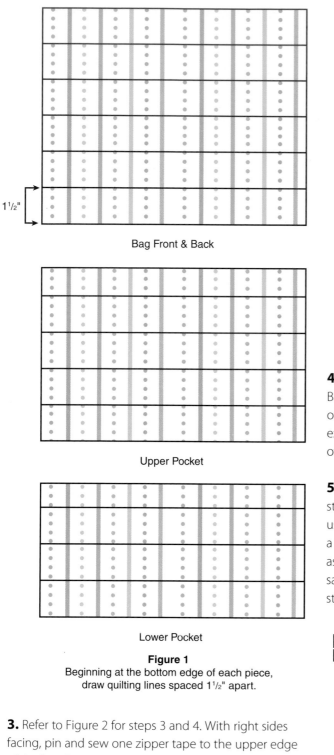

1½"

Bag Front & Back

Upper Pocket

Lower Pocket

Figure 1
Beginning at the bottom edge of each piece,
draw quilting lines spaced 1½" apart.

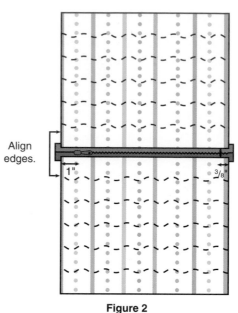

Align edges.

1"

³⁄₈"

Figure 2
Sew zipper to bag front and back.
Press pieces away from the zipper tapes.

3. Refer to Figure 2 for steps 3 and 4. With right sides facing, pin and sew one zipper tape to the upper edge of the bag front. Position so the upper zipper stop is 1 inch from the left cut edge. The lower end of the zipper will extend beyond the right cut edge. Sew the other zipper tape to the upper edge of the bag back in the same manner.

4. Thread a hand-sewing needle and double the thread. Bartack across the zipper teeth ³⁄₈ inch from the cut edge of the fabric to make a new bottom stop. Trim away the excess zipper tape and use needle-nose pliers to break off the plastic teeth beyond the new stop.

5. Position the lower pocket on its batting rectangle and steam-press from the pocket side to adhere the layers (or use temporary spray adhesive to adhere the layers). Apply a zipper tape to the upper edge of the lower pocket as you did for the bag upper front. With the zipper sandwiched between the fabric and the lining rectangle, stitch a scant ¼ inch from the raw edges (Figure 3).

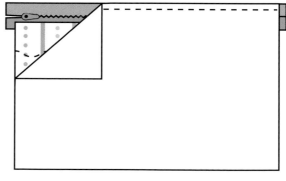

Figure 3
Stitch lining to lower pocket.

6. Turn the lining to the wrong side of the pocket and press, taking care to keep the iron away from the zipper teeth. Machine-baste the layers together a scant ¼ inch from the side and bottom cut edges.

7. Repeat steps 5 and 6 to apply one zipper tape to the upper edge of the upper pocket. Machine-quilt on the marked lines of each pocket.

8. Draw a zipper placement line on the upper pocket 5¼ inches above the lower edge. Position the free edge of the remaining zipper tape on the lower pocket along the placement line. Using a zipper foot, stitch down the center of the zipper tape. Stitch again, close to the edge of the zipper tape (Figure 4).

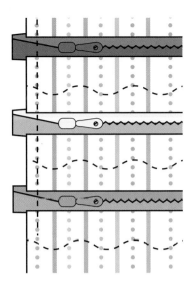

Figure 5
Align edges, lap zipper tapes and baste.

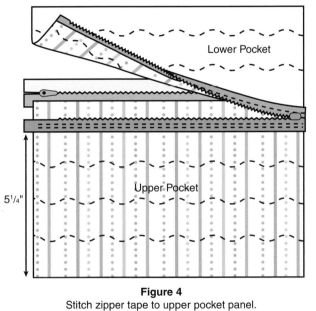

Figure 4
Stitch zipper tape to upper pocket panel.

9. Measure 7 inches up from the bottom edge of the bag front and draw a placement line. Pin and stitch the remaining half of the upper pocket zipper to the bag front as you did for the lower zipper.

10. Align all of the pocket raw edges with the bag front and overlap the zipper tape ends as shown in Figure 5. Machine-baste a scant ¼ inch from the raw edges (Figure 5).

11. With the lining right side against the zipper wrong side, pin and stitch the front and back lining sections to the bag using a scant ¼-inch-wide seam (Figure 6).

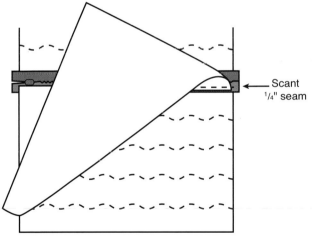

Figure 6
Sew lining to zipper tape and seam allowance only
(not through the bag front).

12. Unzip each zipper halfway. Keeping the linings and uppermost zipper tape free, bring the right sides of the bag front and back together and pin. Stitch the side and bottom edges together ½ inch from the raw edges.

Hand-walk the needle over the zipper teeth and stitch as far as possible. Finish the seam with a few hand stitches near the zipper stop as needed. *Do not force the zipper to flatten, as it may damage the teeth.* Beginning and ending at the level of the middle zipper, grade the bag seam allowances (but not the lining seam allowances) and trim the corners on the diagonal (Figure 7). Bring the right sides of the front lining and back lining together and pin. Stitch, leaving a 7-inch opening in the bottom for turning. If necessary, finish the seam with a few hand stitches near the zipper end stop.

13. Reach inside the lining opening and unzip the top zipper all the way. Turn the bag right side out and push out the lower corners of the bag. Turn under and press the opening edges in the lining and stitch together. ●

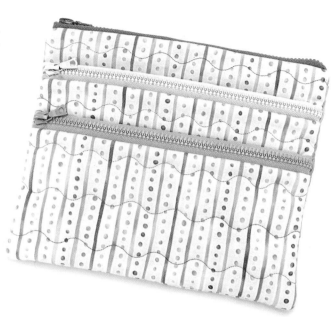

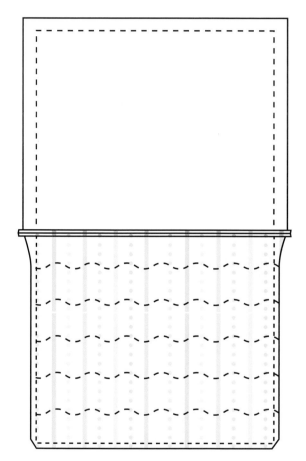

Figure 7
Sew bag and lining pieces together.

Options for Two-Tone Zips

If your local retailer doesn't carry Riri two-tone zippers, locate one who does by visiting www.ririzippers.com. Click on the retailer tab at the far right of the Home screen. Otherwise, you can create a similar look by purchasing three separating sport zippers, each in a different color. Separate the zippers and then mix and match the tapes.

Fabric & Supplies

Page 25: *Oh! Kimono!*—Dove of the East oriental charm; The Warm Co. quilt batting

Page 32: *California Dreamin'*—Blumenthal Craft bamboo handles; Waverly Fabrics Beverly Glen Pink and Rodeo Drive Pink

Page 42: *Denim Delight*—Jitney Flat Braided Handles from Peacock Patterns; The Warm Co. Steam-A-Seam 2

Page 55: *Flower Power*—Covington Industries: Covington Pembroke Plaid and Spectrum "Nina" (floral fabrics; Toray Ultrasuede Soft; Prym-Dritz grommets)

Page 58: *Roll Out the Barrel*—Ultrasuede from Toray Ultrasuede America; Fabric Café Structural Stabilizer; Purrfectly Clear art stamp, and Jacquard textile paint and stamp pad from Purrfections Artistic Wearables

Page 86: *Hobo Sophisticate*—Ultrasuede from Toray Ultrasuede America; Be-Dazzler Stud and Rhinestone setting machine and flat-head studs

Page 98: *Lovely in Lace*—Lace from Cluny Lace Co. Ltd.; William E. Wright Co. decorator cords

Page 156: *Jewels in the Round*—Riri zippers; The Warm Co. batting

Page 170: *Zipper-Dee-Do-Da*—The Warm Co. Soft & Bright needlepunched fleece; Riri zippers

---

Sewing Sources

The following companies provided fabric and/or supplies for projects in this book. If you are unable to locate a product locally, contact the manufacturers listed below for the closest retail or mail-order source in your area.

The Adhesive Products Inc.
www.crafterspick.com

Amazing Designs
www.amazingdesigns.com

Beacon Adhesives
www.beaconadhesives.com

Blumenthal Craft
(800) 553-4158
www.blumenthallansing.com

Cluny Lace Co. Ltd.
www.clunylace.com

Covington Industries
(212) 689-2200
www.covington-industries.com

Dove of the East
(888) 219-0382
www.doveoftheeast.com

Fabric Café
(903) 509-5999
www.fabriccafe.com

Palmer/Pletsch
www.palmerpletsch.com

Peacock Patterns
(877) 266-4681
www.jitneypatterns.com

Prym Dritz
www.prymdritz.com

Purrfections Artistic Wearables
(800) 691-4293
www.purrfections.com

Riri Zippers
www.ririzippers.com

Therm O Web
(847) 520-1140
www.thermoweb.com

Toray Ultrasuede America
(212) 382-1590
www.utrasuede.com

The Warm Co.
(206) 320-9276
www.warmcompany.com

Waverly Fabrics
www.waverly.com

William E. Wright Co.
www.wrights.com

Special Thanks

We would like to thank the talented sewing designers whose work is featured in this collection.

Marta Alto
Bea-Dazzled, 128
Field of Flowers, 68

Annette Bailey
Make It Mandarin, 124

Janice Bullis
Harlequin Romance, 107
Lovely in Lace, 98

Karen Dillon
Little Luxury, 112
Picture This Town Tote, 16
Sling Time, 45
Scarf Trick, 82
Toile Terrific, 11

Nancy Fiedler
Black & Tan & Red
  All Over, 50
Fiesta Fancy, 152
Seeing Double, 28

Stephanie
Corina Goddard
Beaded Amulet, 91
Zipper-Dee-Do-Da, 170

Lucy B. Gray
Anything But Blue, 137
Beachcomber Tote, 36
M-M-M Strawberries!, 142
Scarf Be Ruffled, 102

Linda Turner Griepentrog
A Rose by Any
  Other Name, 132
Denim Delight, 42
Oh! Kimono!, 25

Kelly Lawrence
Pur-Suede Me, 78

Pamela Lindquist
All Buttoned Up, 115
Aloha Fantasy Tote, 6
Pretty as a Posy, 160

Judy Murrah
Triangles All Around, 20

Pauline Richards
Jewels in the Round, 156

Julie Weaver
Roll It Up, 165

Barbara Weiland
Flap Happy, 73
Lacy Bridal Wristlet, 95
Plaid She Said!, 62

Lynn Weglarz
Beauty in the Bag, 148

Hope Yoder
Something Borrowed,
  Something Blue, 118

Carol Zentgraf
California Dreamin', 32
Flower Power, 55
Hobo Sophisticate, 86
Roll Out the Barrel, 58